Maya Yoga

Sloane Dulban
2nd Rec from
Ron Stewart
June 2014
quoted on RM
site

Maya Yoga

Longchenpa's *Finding Comfort and Ease in Enchantment*

A Book of Dzogchen Precepts

Introduction and Translation by
Keith Dowman

Vajra Publications

Published by
Vajra Publications
Jyatha, Thamel,
P.O. Box 21779, Kathmandu, Nepal
Tel.: 977-1-4220562, Fax: 977-1-4246536
e-mail: bidur_la@mos.com.np
www.vajrabooks.com.np

Distributor
Vajra Books
Kathmandu, Nepal

ISBN 978-9937-506-45-8

Printed in Nepal

Other Titles by Keith Dowman

Natural Perfection (originally published as
Old Man Basking in the Sun)
Eye of the Storm
The Flight of the Garuda
The Sacred Life of Tibet
Power-places of Kathmandu
Boudhanath: The Great Stupa
Masters of Enchantment
The Power-places of Central Tibet: The Pilgrim's Guide
Masters of Mahamudra
Sky-Dancer: The Secret Life and Songs of the Lady Yeshe Tsogyel
The Nyingma Icons.
The Divine Madman: The Life and Songs of Drukpa Kunley
The Legend of the Great Stupa
Calm and Clear: A Manual of Buddhist Meditation

See also www.keithdowman.net

Homage to Guru Rinpoche and the Vajra Dakini!

Dedicated to the late Dr Herbert Guenther

We think of the key, each in his prison
thinking of the key, each confirms a prison.
T.S Eliot, *The Waste Land*

We shall not cease from exploration
And the end of all our exploring
Will be to arrive where we started
And know the place for the first time.
T.S.Eliot, *Little Gidding*

CONTENTS

PREFACE

Longchen Rabjampa was perhaps the greatest mind to walk in the Land of the Snows. *Finding Comfort and Ease in Enchantment*, published under the title *Maya Yoga*, is the third volume in his *Trilogy of Finding Comfort and Ease*. The first volume is *Finding Comfort and Ease in the Nature of Mind* and the second *Finding Comfort and Ease in Meditation*. I make no apology for another translation of one of Longchenpa's seminal Dzogchen texts. Each generation of translators makes its own interpretation of such important works, each building upon the next, until a final authoritative version is reached. Even now another generation of translators has assimilated its forebear's expertise, seemingly by cognitive osmosis, and has made a giant leap towards those final versions. I hope that this translation may be of use to them; but my main purpose is to represent the precepts whereby the mystical view of maha-ati can be recognized and its experiential understanding become available to all.

The publication in 1980 of Dr Herbert Guenther's translation of *The Trilogy of Finding Comfort and Ease* by Tarthang Tulku's Dharma Publishing under the title *Kindly Bent to Ease Us* was a crucial event in the publication of Dzogchen texts. It initiated a new phase of Dzogchen translation and offered a revised vocabulary for it. Concomitantly it provided a rationalization of the Vajrayana praxis that until then had been couched in simplistic, devotional terms. To some that was a retrograde movement, insofar as it provided sustenance for the intellect, whereas this very intellect was the principal obstacle to 'feeling' the lamas' meaning. Dr Guenther's translation of the title, the strange and evocative *Kindly Bent to Ease Us*, seemed to bring into doubt the validity of the very view it presented, to characterize it as provisional, to present a functional yet perverted sadhana. For others it deepened an intuitive insight into the nature of mind by providing an added psychological and philosophical dimension to the vocabulary of Dzogchen poetry. To some it brought disappointment by its use of the exoteric academic terminology of phenomenology that here in some places explicated but there in others tended to obscure Longchenpa's meaning—it was aimed at the philosopher-academic by a philosopher-academic rather than at the existential yogi or yogini. Those readers were appalled by the absence in the translation of the poetic power and beauty that marks Longchenpa's work, although even Dr Guenther could not but fall occasionally into some poetic conceits that were poignantly reminiscent of the lyrical nature of the original Tibetan. To others it established the Vajrayana vision in contemporary western cultural and philosophical tradition. Other readers were delighted to find their intellect challenged to grasp the immensity of the vast Dzogchen vision.

This critique is not intended to demean Dr Guenther's work, but rather to distinguish it as cutting edge and controversial. This exacting, impeccable scholar had already made an invaluable contribution to Buddhist studies, both theoretical and practical, before the publication of Kindly *Bent*. For me, personally, his *Philosophy and Psychology in the Abhidharma* provided a concise and profound theoretical basis for a shamatha retreat in Almora, India, in 1967, and *The Jewel Ornament of Liberation* was a constant inspirational friend during ngondro practice in the following years. In subsequent titles Dr Guenther achieved giant steps in Tibetan translation and elucidation of technical terminology and thereby enlightened an entire generation of academics that were otherwise irked by the simplistic devotional language of Tibetan tulkus barely conversant with the wonderful subtleties, nuances and ambiguities of the infinitely flexible English language.

Certainly, in *Kindly Bent to Ease Us* Dr Guenther provided a crib whereby his students could read the Tibetan while remaining aware of the metaphysical denotations and the parallels in academic phenomenology. It provided an excellent prop for any further translation—perhaps he had that purpose in mind. Some of his English equivalents of technical Tibetan terms, however, have become redundant like his 'creative imagination' (for *sgom pa*), or 'limpid clearness and consummate perspicacity' (for *byang chub sems*). Sometimes in my opinion Dr Guenther erred in his reading of the Tibetan. Occasionally he spins the meaning to conform to preconceived rational assumptions, thereby losing sight of Longchenpa's ulterior intentions. Frequently his heavy-handed treatment of common Buddhist terms obscures the sense of a phrase. But what is perhaps the most invidious tendency in his translation is to spin the work in the direction of an objective philosophical exposition, at the expense of the subtle and secret dimension of magical poetry. His is an interesting point of view and one that may have induced many academic seekers to delve further into Tibetan Buddhism. But Longchenpa's aim was not to provide a seamless monograph on the nature of mind, but rather to provide lucid precepts for those already on the Vajrayana path, illuminating them with his own unique and profound experiential understanding.

In spite of these shortcomings, in *Kindly Bent* and his other works, Herbert Guenther made a towering contribution to the study of Tibetan Buddhism. Besides students of Buddhism, innumerable devotees, yogis and yoginis, in the western world have cause to thank him for his life work. But one other thing remains to be said, which may be best framed as a question. Did Dr Guenther bring a prior intuition of the nature of mind to his work or did his work induce a realization of that buddha-nature? Whichever way the question is answered we have reason to celebrate his understanding. For these reasons I have dedicated this book to him.

In this translation of *Finding Comfort and Ease in Enchantment* I have tried to follow a middle way between a reflection of technical meaning and interpretive poetry in order to provide access to those who would use the text as a manual. Use of a manual of Vajrayana precepts is facilitated by authorisation and elucidation from a master of the literary lineage: the ritual of *lung* provides that.

It is interesting to note that *The Trilogy of Finding Comfort and Ease* is becoming the most renowned of Longchenpa's many works. Dr Guenther began the trend of course with *Kindly Bent to Ease Us*. In the year 2000 the Dalai Lama taught the second volume of the trilogy in France and his commentary and the translation have been published by Wisdom Publications under the title *Mind in Comfort and Ease*. Longchenpa's voluminous auto-commentary on the trilogy called *The Great Chariot* is in process of translation and will be published also by Wisdom Publications. *Finding Comfort and Ease in Enchantment* describes the culmination of the graduated path described in the first two volumes of the trilogy and thus lends itself to the radical view.

I offer my thanks to David Boaz, John S. Richardson and Jeremiah Weser for their invaluable assistance in the editing process.

Keith Dowman
At the Great Stupa of Boudhanath
Kathmandu
Iron Tiger New Year, February 2010

INTRODUCTION

As the tradition of Dzogchen has gained ground in the West, it appears to have produced two quite distinct responses. At best, a recognition of the natural state of being—the nature of mind as known in direct experience of it—is induced. Taking 'the position of consequence', yanking themselves up by their own bootstraps as it were, those who know the Great Perfection simply by hearing an introduction to it recognize the spaciousness of pure presence. Then another response, from people who approach reality timorously, is awe and devotion. They meet the lineage-holding lamas like petitioners in the court of an oriental despot, knocking their heads on the floor, begging for a crumb from the high table. Then transported to a high level of radiance through the lama's grace, the supplicant basks in splendour until the moment arrives to return to the source for more.

The first response enables and enacts the immediate recognition of radical Dzogchen while the second reaction is a precursor of the gradual path of latter-day, elaborate or cultural, Dzogchen. The first relies upon existential experience and the precepts of atiyoga contained in the ancient texts and the second depends upon a relationship with the father-guru, upon mahayoga meditation practice and the religious life. In the first case an assumption is made that the nondual awareness of pure presence is the natural state of being and that nothing can be done to attain what is already reality. In the second case, the least confident and most humble of our assumptions about ourselves is that we are hopelessly lost in the mire of this birth yet we have glimpsed a bright light out there, far away in the distance, and we have identified an honest guide able and willing to direct us on the path towards it. The view on the second path—that we live in the relative world of shadows and seek the absolute realm of light—is in apparent discord with the radical Dzogchen view—that we are already in that inexpressible nondual reality in which absolute and relative are one. The difference seems as basic as that between chalk and cheese; the gradual and the immediate paths are incommensurate.

In *Finding Comfort and Ease in Enchantment* Longchenpa allays the suspicion that the gradual and immediate paths are mutually exclusive, and that people from different worlds entertain them. Rather, the difference appears to be between different personality types recognising the same reality but from different perspectives, describing the same experience in radically different terms leading to different responses and different approaches. This distinction is surely quite superficial like the difference between the two sides of a single coin. In the view of Longchenpa in this treatise the gradual and the immediate paths are the two sides of that same coin; they may be as far away as the earth is from the sky but they complement each other. If mahayoga with its elaborate ritual meditation practices of visualization and recitation is taken as the method of partial fulfilment of the goal of the gradual path and atiyoga is seen as the source of the precepts of immediate realization, then likewise mahayoga and atiyoga complement each other and on the graduated path may be performed either in series or in parallel. In *The Trilogy of Finding Comfort and Ease,* the first two volumes focus upon mahayoga and elements of the gradual path while *Finding Comfort and Ease in Enchantment* provides the keys to immediate realization and the radical view. In this introduction I have tried to highlight the atiyoga aspect. The admission of the unity of gradual and immediate allows the humility to admit to feet of clay and to the function of purification. It also allows the confidence based in the undeniable existential experience of Garab Dorje's first incisive precept that is conducive to maintenance of the secret praxis of *maha-ati.*

So this short treatise of Longchenpa is a manual of primal awareness in the great Dzogchen tradition of Tibetan Buddhism. It provides the precepts that may instantly illuminate the buddha-reality that is our ordinary everyday experience. It asserts that we are presently under the spell of magical illusion and that by recognition of that fact we are, instantaneously, released from a conceptual cage into an enchanting reality that is pure pleasure itself. This is a manual defining human life lived as enchantment, where the ignorance of delusory samsara proves to be the insight into the Great Perfection of illusion. We begin in the heat of desirous attachment to our egoistic selves, and merely through recognition of our deluded condition, chilled out in the birthless and deathless space of reality, we find respite and release in the magical display of our everyday life.

The working title of this book has been *Chilling Out in Enchantment*, a rendering of the Tibetan title that expresses the nature of the cool contemplation behind all our moment-to-moment twenty-four/seven experience. It is such contemplation that provides the sense of vast mystery, exhilarating and uplifting, to release us from the heaviness and density, the confusion and pettiness, of samsaric existence. That title also carries the sense of a resolution of the dilemmas of dualism in a respite of relaxed, carefree refreshment, basking in the sun of intrinsic awareness. Through the precepts contained in this manual, published as *Finding Comfort and Ease in Enchantment* in deference to the scholars who have worked on the text before me, we familiarize ourselves with the natural, illusory, state of being, this state of wonderment, living a selfless phantasm of sensory pleasure and aesthetic appreciation.

This book, therefore, is about the nondual reality of Dzogchen as magical illusion, as *maya*, and I will use that exalted, profound, vernacular Sanskrit word in this introduction to evoke the magic and mystery, the light and the love, of Dzogchen. Maya, then, is the very nature of Dzogchen, nondual reality itself. In *Finding Comfort and Ease in Enchantment* the Tibetan master Longchenpa—a second buddha—in eight chapters of high Tibetan poetry elucidates and evokes that reality while exhorting us to recognize its immanence through the Dzogchen precepts of atiyoga. The precepts that govern the recognition of the maya of everyday existence, the maya of ordinary mind, are woven like a magic spell into the elucidation of the eight famous analogies of maya collated by the great Indian pandita Nagarjuna—another second buddha. All our experience of life is like last night's dream; it is like a magic show of an infallible master magician; it is like optical illusion; it is like a mirage in the desert; it is like the reflection of the moon in water; it is like an echo reverberating between mountain crags; it is like a cloud land which we call the city of the gandharvas; and it is like an apparitional emanation, like a phantom or a ghost.

Thus this book is a manual of atiyoga that opens the door into Dzogchen's nondual reality, the reality of maya—magical illusion, happiness.

Maya and its Aspects

First, then, let us look closely at Longchenpa's notion of maya. In the first sentences of the work, in his chapter on dream, maya assumes two aspects. The first is the basic immaculate maya that is our original, natural, state of being. It is this nondual maya of our self-illuminating awareness that constitutes our innate three-dimensional buddha-being inseparable from its intrinsic primal awareness. This unitary reality presents itself spontaneously and perfectly in every instant of the here and now as an integral part of the cosmic whole, like a hologram. This is the maya of the Great Perfection and in its nondual awareness it lies beyond the intellect.

The second aspect is the delusory maya created by the intellect, known as the maya of false conception. This maya arises within the space of immaculate maya as a loss of the natural intrinsic awareness of our original state of being, and we call it ignorance. This maya unfolds as the wheel of life. It is embodied as one of the six mythic modes of being (or six psychological types) each in its own mental environment. Here the laws of karma operate, and according to our activity in our own personal environment we suffer the pleasure and pain of our daily existence. As the primal awareness of immaculate maya is increasingly adulterated by attachment to the daily round, so the function of mind that we call the intellect increases in its capacity to structure and differentiate a reality that is vast unstructured space. The nondual reality of our immaculate original state manifests as the dualistic space-time world that we know in our everyday experience and which physicists and psychologists examine in their laboratories.

This maya of our ordinary experience rests upon the structure that our intellect imposes. This is a diverse and complex system of concepts and beliefs that not only determines the quality and nature of our experience but also of the natural, seemingly external, world. This belief system and the maya of experience that it manifests, however, is never cloven from the vast expanse of compassionate clear light in which it arises. The 'maya of false conception' and the 'basic immaculate maya' of our natural state are one. The Dzogchen precepts in this manual provide the means of recognition and realization of this great truth. Longchenpa's eight analogies provide the doorway back into this our intrinsic natural state of being. Recognition of the basic immaculate maya defines the immediate radical pathless path of Dzogchen while the maya of false conception implies a graduated structured path.

Given that our experience of life has provided a direct intuitive recognition of the nature of reality as maya, and that our concepts and belief systems, although intellectually conceived, comprehend that the purpose of our embodied being is to recognize the unity of our basic immaculate maya and the maya of false concepts, Longchenpa proposes and focuses upon four particular instances of maya. The first is the actuality of our lives that is the starting point and the goal of the transformation that is realized by experiential recognition of our true nature. The nature of this actuality is illustrated by the analogy of a magic show. Just as a magician contrives the illusion of an event out of light and sound—*son et lumière*—wherein the stage props of the illusion remain unchanged, so the delusive, spectacular, maya emerges out of the fundament of the clear light of the nature of mind. This clear light is in turn illustrated by the metaphor of the mirror that reflects endlessly yet remains untainted by the images that appear upon its surface.

The second instance of maya is the delusory, dualistic world that we are convinced is real and in which we believe. We suppose ourselves to be an objective body-mind, an ego, existing in a material world that is separate, out there, independent of the mind that perceives it. That comprises the polluted, contaminated, maya of samsara.

The third instance is the maya that is a method of decontamination, a technical contemplative means to recognize the nature of mind, an agenda that turns back the ever proliferating elaborations of the intellect upon themselves. This maya comprises religious—or psychological—dharma practice as the path.

Longchenpa's fourth functional aspect is the maya of primordially pure pristine awareness. This is indistinguishable from the basic immaculate maya. It arises with complete ego-loss—surrender—and it subverts all sense of distinction between subjective inner and objective outer perception. Here the mother clear light (of our natural state of being) and the son clear light (of the individual's existential realization) coalesce and the starting point is recognized as the goal.

The maya that is our experience of life is like a dream, a magic show, an echo, a mirage or an apparition and by these analogies we shall know it. The recognition of these four instances of maya, on the other hand, as the four principal or functional categories of maya on the path of Vajrayana, identifies and clarifies the form in which maya arises—and brings it all back home. Longchenpa dwells on these distinctions in *Magical Show: The Second Analogy*, which is perhaps the most important chapter in the text. The first instance of maya is its actuality understood through the initiatory intuition of the nature of mind. In these luminous moments of insight when we stand with the buddhas; when the vast spaciousness of the ground of being is identified with the primal awareness that is intrinsic to every sensory perception, internal and external; when the nondual reality of being can be extrapolated and pictured as a magic show and the cognitive aspect described as the clear, immutable, expanse that is like the surface of a mirror: in those very moments we realize the ground of transformation out of which samsara and nirvana emerge. This is our starting point. Still cloaked in the delusions of ignorance we are fully aware of the pristine perfection of our natural state of being. Here we are fully persuaded of the perfectibility of our embodied existence. Our lives, forever changed, can never be the same. These are initiatory moments that arise fortuitously, adventitiously, in the mindstream of the individual. They are represented in the Dzogchen rituals called 'introduction to the nature of mind' or 'pointing out instruction' or 'the fourth initiation'.

Although such moments of timeless awareness are transformative in our experience of them, the unremitting habitual tendencies ingrained by dualistic experience through the history of the human race and through our own endless succession of rebirths—through 'genetic' and 'personal' karma—we relapse into the dualistic world of samsara. Samsara is composed of an amalgam of belief systems the product of which Longchenpa terms 'contaminated maya'. As projections upon the vast spaciousness of being we believe that there are objective 'things' out there in the external world with a solid 'real' existence and that those entities possess undeniable fixed attributes. We believe that the sun is a star in the Milky Way and that the planet Earth revolves around it, rotating upon its axis, with a satellite moon. We believe that embodied sentient beings live on planet earth, moving, eating and breathing, copulating and communicating, conscious of their environment and inner lives. We believe in an underlying integrity that fixes both the outer and the inner universes in a given, objectively and fundamentally real—true—structure. We may or may not conceive or believe that integral factor is God or the godhead and believe in Him, but we certainly do assume a fixed order in the cosmos. And certainly we believe in a compound of name, form, energies, consciousness and proclivities as a self, an ego, an objectively existent being that is born from a mother's womb and which develops though age to experience sickness and finally death.

We 'believe' in the veracity of our sensory experience. Although we know first that every sensory perception is contrived by the structure (the shape and form) and the function ('seeing', 'hearing') of the sense organ as sensory stimuli impinge upon it, and, second, by the projective and interpretive cognitive functions of the intellect, believing those perceptions to be real we reify them as objectively existent physical/mental reality. These karmically induced chronic habits of interpretation and projection may be termed 'genetic' insofar as the basic beliefs about the external world are determined by the structure and function of the psycho-organism itself. Or the notion of 'past lives' from the very inception of the species of *homo sapiens* can be evoked to indicate the unconscious depth of the psyche that produces the interpretive/projective images by which we 'know' the external world—its images, colours and shapes. Upon that fundamental structure—shared by all human beings—personal karmic experience determines the specifics of sensory perception, prioritisation of features and detail, whether the sensation is to be rejected or accepted, its emotional tone, its mental environment according to the six fold mythic categorisation of the Buddhist tradition (human, animal, divine, demonic, ghost-like and hellish) and so on. All that projective, interpretive and selective mental activity is the work of the intellect and the constructs, concepts and thoughts that it entails are preconscious—subliminal—'belief', and we are attached to it.

Our ordinary experience, in between moments of recognition of the nature of mind, is the actuality of maya polluted by intellectual belief. The third functional aspect of maya is the illusion of decontamination, the delusion of an intentional sadhana, a graduated path, an intellectual thrust supported by a conducive lifestyle that eradicates the inveterate tendencies that relentlessly structure the immediate illusion of our experience. On a superficial, preparatory level, we can begin by shaking the bigotry of the intellect by undermining its logical certainties, its habits and presumptions. That implies a rejection—or at least a 'phenomenological bracketing'—of the overt product of the senses. The crass naïve materialist thumping the table and saying, 'And isn't this real?' is in denial of the ineluctable dominant cognitive component of every perception. Indeed in every cognitive event our specifically personal beliefs about the reality of the external world are undermined by the logic of variable sensory experience under evolving conditions. The subjectivity of our deeper, hidden, preconscious, common, shared beliefs about the external world and its presumed immutable reality are easily refuted by the proofs offered by the scanning electron microscope and by quantum theory and particle physics in the field of objective investigation. We can start the process of a reassessment of conventional, space-time pragmatic reality by assimilating the message of some contemporary art forms—painting and sculpture for instance—and some motion pictures. Then turning inward in discursive analytical meditation we can search for an essence that is substantial and permanent and yet find only emptiness.

On a deeper, subtler and more effective level of decontamination, we can utilize the uniquely Dzogchen yogas of existential deconstruction. Every sensory perception whatsoever is a 'light-form' contaminated by innate mental propensities to concretize itself as an external entity—an alien 'other'—and to react to it with positive or negative attachment. By focussing upon it as an aspect of pure light the 'object' is deconstructed cognitively until only the light of cognition remains, leaving us nothing to hold on to, nothing to be attached to, nothing to reinforce the preconceived notion of an 'external' object cognized by an 'internal' perceiver. Turning within, the same yoga is applied to thoughts and emotions—thoughts in particular—which are also and more obviously experienced as light. In that way all beliefs manifesting as thought-forms are rendered non-affective and effete, to be self-reflexively released at the instant of arising. The Dzogchen view provides a cognitive dialectic that involuntarily reduces dualistic thought and its forms—polarities, dichotomies, dualisms—to the elemental unitary light of primordial awareness (*rigpa*). If our experience of the nature of mind is in fact an indication of our original, natural, state of being then the rolling snowball effect is now activated and an unmediated process that deconstructs existential reality continues to overwhelm the seemingly implacable steamrolling logic of karmic propensity. It is axiomatic that the Dzogchen view is symbiotically coincident with Dzogchen meditation, or rather Dzogchen nonmeditation. This nonmeditation is the ultimate instrument of decontamination. It is indicated in the Dzogchen view as non-action as opposed to any contrived mental action during meditation sitting. It is glossed also as 'non-deliberate activity'. Non-action allows relaxation into the primordial purity of the ground of being where primal awareness illuminates the delusory maya that has then become immaculate maya. There is no technical meditation instruction that contrives the state of relaxation. Non-action cannot be fabricated. No controller exists who can set himself up for dissolution and self-destruction. The surrender that culminates in dissolution is only reached through the precepts of the Dzogchen view that are truly no-precepts.

This third aspect of maya, the technical illusion, can be pictured as the magical illusion of Dzogchen yogis and yoginis striving to resolve the fantasies and paradoxes that the intellect creates. Every technique of sadhana has a starting point, a path and a goal; a beginning, a middle and an end; preparation, application, 'seeing' and familiarization. In the context of this Cutting Through phase (*trekcho*), 'preparation' may refer to repeated momentary experience of the nature of mind; 'application' to the gradual assimilation of mundane experience to the nature of mind; 'seeing' to insight into the sameness of every situation that provides a continuity of unbroken moments of pure presence; and finally 'familiarization' to the constant presence of pure presence where karma is exhausted.

It may be appropriate here to note how the paradigm of Tibetan Buddhist sadhana was assimilated by the psychedelic movement of the 'sixties. Mind-altering substances replaced simply-sitting and the processes of creative and fulfilment meditation as the arena in which the nature of mind was recognized. While it is evident that recognition is only momentary, permitted only for the duration of the effect of the chemical, such experience can act as a touchstone upon which reality may be gauged in an ongoing sadhana wherein conviction of the 'truth' of all experience is recognized, allowing confidence in reflexive release to arise. Psychedelics remain an uncertain method of attaining a powerful experience of recognition of the ground of being. But like psychopathic states and near-death experience, they seem to be able to induce a foretaste of the nature of mind. Particularly under the rubric of shamanism they should not be rejected or belittled, especially in cultures, like the Mexican and South American, in which the tradition of substance-induced psychedelic mysticism has existed for many generations.

The fourth functional aspect of maya is what remains experientially after all belief in any substantial reality whatsoever has been expunged. When our nonmeditation, our insight into the nature of mind, reveals the wondrous essential truth that the external world and our experience of it, and the inner world of thought and emotion, is all contrived by the intellect, that it has no substantial existence, at that time the understanding of maya dawns. Both inner and the outer are illusory. It is all magical display. It is unitary maya.

The Real and The True

It is a basic human karmic propensity to conceive the field of our experience as real and true. We believe in the reality of the objective external world and of our subjective, personal, inner world. Certainly one of Longchenpa's aims in *Finding Comfort and Ease in Enchantment* is to convince us of the falsity, the untruth, the unreality, of that belief. In common usage what is 'true' is accurate fact, confirmed by public perception (intersubjective verification), or logically consistent, scientifically attested, reasonable and rational argument. In our application of the Dzogchen precepts given by Longchenpa in *Finding Comfort and Ease in Enchantment* we are obliged to deny the factuality of our dualistic experience. We cannot break through into the intrinsic spaciousness of our mindstream unless we suspend our belief in conventional reality as real and true. Moral truth, scientific truth, assumptions about the actual content of our sensory experience, all must be subsumed under the heading of 'lies', 'falsehood', 'unreality'. The entire belief system by which we relate professionally, socially and sexually, domestically and personally, must be undermined, deconstructed and rendered ineffectual. Every belief system is hypothetical, a superficial construction, capable of replacement by an alternative set of beliefs. It is all delusion. It is deceiving, duplicitous, spurious fiction. It is a lie. In that way, by rejecting fact as 'true', we begin to relieve ourselves of the density and heaviness, not to say bigotry, of our beliefs about the nature of reality.

In religious culture 'truth' has a deeper meaning. No longer dependant upon intellectual validity or proof, no longer a function of intellectual belief, it could be defined as an intuition of a constant, unchanging, blissful reality, or wisdom. That 'truth' is god, a meaning familiar to those who have heard the chant of Hindu pallbearers on their way to the cremation ground—'*Ram Ram satya hai*!' 'God is truth!' they cry over and over. Likewise the Muslims cry of '*Allah Akbar*!' affirms that God is 'truth'. This truth that is God is the substance of belief and fulfils our craving for security, something solid to hold on to and to cling to, something seemingly graspable to which we can attach ourselves. That truth may be projected outside upon an external entity or internalized as a soul or *jiva*, an aspect of god within. The prophets—Jewish, Muslim, Christian or Hindu—have verbally interpreted that truth as God's law and formulated a moral dogma and discipline—and a priesthood. When we submit to that truth and its entire, inherently limited, belief system, we accept the structures that it imposes upon the intrinsic spaciousness of mind and involuntarily we become advocates of its limitations. The principal of those imagined structures is belief in a self, an ego, a person, and that person intellectually emanates the entire dualistic structure of separate subject and object, inside and outside, I and it, me and her, mine and theirs, good and evil, right and wrong and so on. And thus nonduality is divisively dualized—conflicted—and we are caught in the god-trap. Religious culture is contaminated maya.

Of the many precepts that *Finding Comfort and Ease in Enchantment* provides, those that exhort us to see maya as delusion predominate. We should remember here that in his characterisation of experience as delusory, Longchenpa is not attempting an objective worldview, a philosophy that describes man in his environment. Rather, he is giving us the tools whereby we can return to the natural state of being that is our home. In order to do that, we need to be consistently rigorous in our application of the precepts. Everything that is, all our experience up to and including mystical experience of the divine, is untrue: it is invalid, inauthentic; it is falsehood, a lie; it is fiction; it is spurious or counterfeit. It is unreal. Thus in ordinary parlance when we say 'That is true!' in response to a statement of fact we should be aware that in fact we are asserting the truth of delusion. 'Fact', insofar as it is merely a partial truth, is always a lie even in conventional reality. How more so is it a falsehood when every aspect and feature in our experience is truly or factually a deceptive untruth, a part of the Great Lie that is our multidimensional experience!

We should also be aware that intensity of belief or experience is no barometer of truth. An overwhelming epiphany of the nature of God—'to be reborn in God'—does not make it authentic or true, although it may be unique in our experience. Profound religious experience simply provides an example of the magnificence and beauty of maya and demonstrates its capacity to mesmerize and enthral. Such experience is also zero-dimensional, like brushing one's teeth. Likewise, when at certain stages of life specific hormones saturate the body-mind, and undeniable attitudes and feelings dominate our being and we are moved to extraordinarily intense love or hate, to 'true love' or to fratricidal war, and we have no choice but to copulate with our sisters or to kill our brothers, there is no 'truth' in our motivation or our actions, it is all maya—delusion, falsehood, a lie. Love, for example, whether it lodges upon a person, an animal, an object, or god, so long as we believe in its validity is always and only fiction, becoming 'true' always and only when it is recognized as an illusory ephemeral figment of mind.

We are tempted to accept this illusory world by the universal dualistic appeal of pleasure and pain and we become attached to it. Certainly we become attached to specific partial features of that samsara as 'this house and car' or 'that house and car', 'this partner' or 'that partner' and 'my career' and 'my country' and so on, acceptance of delusion as truth follows like a cart after the horse. We may accept and suffer all our experience as delusory emanation of maya and yet still maintain, for instance, that the only 'true love' is the spontaneity of compassion that perceives all as equal and does not focus upon or reside in any particular person or place—buddha-love. When this dualism of relative and absolute becomes so beguiling that our attachments are intractable, we should remember that the didactic distinction in Buddhist logic between conventional (or relative) truth and absolute truth is also a formulation of the intellect, another final trick of maya. The two truths are perhaps better known as 'the two lies'. We know by universal agreement—as part of our social contract—that conventional truth has only limited validity and that what we assert as true is only valid in its context of rational causality and then only so long as it is useful. That is pragmatic truth. And, whether, like the Hindus, we accept a transcendental truth that we call 'God' who is eternal, authentic and righteous, or whether like the Buddhists our definition of ultimate truth depends upon the notion of emptiness, or as in the formulations of secular humanism upon scientific materialism, we still postulate further a reality that is absolute. Longchenpa dismisses such dualisms as constructs of the delusive mind; he often points at the nondual nature of mind and unitary maya. Conceptual projections are a seductive strategy of maya to impose a pragmatic intellectual distinction—a cloak—

upon what in direct experience is utterly beyond the intellect, inconceivable, inexpressible and unimaginable.

Reality lies beyond the dualism of truth and falsehood. We may use the contrived verbal constructions of 'untruth' and 'unreality' in our meditation to shake lose the gross tentacles of belief that metastasize throughout our being, but when we begin to recognize the nature of that reality as not other than the clear light of experience, even the formula that defines that reality as beyond both truth and falsehood, fact and fiction, the authentic and the inauthentic, valid and invalid, and, finally, reality and illusion itself, is made redundant. Such is the profound Dzogchen dialectic.

The crucial point in this Dzogchen view is that maya is a nondual experience. Maya is the starting point, which is our own circumstantial situation, our personal samsara, recognized as the ground of being out of which it arises. It is, therefore, also the path and the goal. Maya is the unitary container and contents, the chalice and the elixir. The container cannot be conceived of by the contents—only intuited or 'felt'. Unitary maya is aware of itself, intrinsically or spontaneously aware, and that awareness is intrinsic pure presence. Following Longchenpa's exhortation in his meditation precepts to regard all experience as illusion, we are left suspended in the timeless basic space of maya. Striving towards the goal of deconstruction of the intellectually contrived dualistic world through the actualization of these precepts, effortlessly, involuntarily, we arrive at the goal that has been present from the beginning. The starting point is recognized as the goal. The implication is that since recognition is the sole prerequisite nothing can be done to achieve accomplishment of this nondual maya. To regard every situation as a magic show is simply to relax into it and enjoy it. Thus—non-action. The difficulty—the impossibility—of verbalising nondual maya directly is surmounted by the use of the eight similes.

Maya Yoga as Atiyoga

First, in order to recognize the reality of release from the dualistic world there is an initial necessity to realize that we are stuck in it. But that dualistic recognition itself is a doorway out of the relative world, into nonduality—out of contaminated maya into immaculate maya. That recognition is an understanding of where we are and where we want to be as identical. In that understanding the relative has dissolved and the nondual is realized; the relative has gone—it never existed—and only nondual maya remains. That nondual maya we may call the unity of relative and absolute or the natural state of being. The recognition of the limitations of our subject/object dichotomy places our consciousness in the arena of atiyoga where there is only the thinnest, subtle, most transparent distinction between knowing and not knowing. In fact, both knowing and not knowing are pure presence: knowing is pure presence itself and not knowing is the effulgence of pure presence, its energetic expression. That realization is inherent in the recognition of our dualistic situation as such. Another way to say it is that samsara is nirvana only when we recognize samsara as a state of suffering. Nirvana lies in the clear seeing—in the clarity—not in the specific form that is seen when suffering and anxiety colour the entire spectrum of possibility.

The specific forms that appear belong to our karmically determined lifestyle. If we are committed to the bodhisattva ideal, that lifestyle should be denominated as the gradual path. The actual form of the lifestyle is immaterial so long as it is recognized as the vehicle by which the Great Perfection is realized moment by moment. That is to say there is no specific discipline or conduct preferable to any other, or any lifestyle that facilitates the realization of the nature of mind more than any other. Insofar as all conduct is karmically determined until all karma is exhausted, whatever arises is an appropriate karma. Thus the gradual path may be religious or secular, consisting of the lifestyle of a monk, yogi or layman.

It is irrelevant which persona clothes our body-mind or which role we play in the drama of life—a lesson taught clearly in the Mahamudra tradition of the Mahasiddhas where any trade or profession could be used as the vehicle of transformation. In practice, however, in the Dzogchen arena we often find that the monk, yogin and layman are partial to the bias of their own karmic proclivities. Particularly, in the monastic environment the monk is closely attached to his religious activities and he tends to high-profile the disciplined compassionate approach described in the Mahayana sutras. The Dalai Lama and the Geluk Dzogchen lineage fit naturally into the monkish category, but there are many Nyingma lamas educated first in the monastery and then in a dharma academy, for example, who also advocate the sutra-oriented approach of discipline (*vinaya*) and concentration-meditation (*shamatha*) as preliminary training for maha-ati. This generates a biased view and a judgmental attitude to the conduct of the layman, particularly the secular layman. The layman who is free of the dualistic vows of Buddhist praxis, however, has greater space, perhaps, in which a true, undiscriminating, anonymous, unselfconscious Dzogchen awareness may grow.

Whereas the monk, yogi or layman will tend to stress the form of the graduated path that he cultivates, identifying with the Dzogchen path as such, he must know that the form is irrelevant in the light of nondual realization. So long as he is unaware of the nondual he will strive to attain the goals of his particular gradual path. Insofar as pure presence dominates, the goals, forms and vows of his progressive path become irrelevant. To put it simply, in the Dzogchen view the difference between the gradual and immediate paths is the same difference between the relative and the absolute truth—there is none. The gradual path allows cultivation, refinement and enhancement of form and style, which may be considered 'improvement' and 'progress' but anyhow—with or without 'practice'—it is the creativity, or effulgence, of pure presence. The radical Dzogchen view of atiyoga assumes the nonduality of spaciousness and intrinsic awareness as pure presence and in the timeless moment of the here and now never—never—can the twain be separated. Form is emptiness and emptiness is form.

Nonduality is the nature of reality and relative truth is the ignorant delusion that is subsumed by it. As the tradition maintains, the distinction between relative and absolute is a delusive function of the intellect and in reality the two truths cannot be parted. If we make the gradual path distinct from what we could call the nondual path we introduce an impossible dualism into the Dzogchen view. At the time of assimilating the first of the three parts of Longchenpa's trilogy, *Finding Comfort and Ease in the Nature of Mind,* which deals with the starting point wherein the aspects of the enlightened mind are progressively recognized, the danger lies in forgetting the Dzogchen view and our own initiatory experience. Likewise, if we are not familiar with the Dzogchen view, if we are not constantly aware of existential experience of the nature of mind, during meditation retreat, as described in the second part of the trilogy, we will not know nonmeditation. In this third part of the trilogy treating enchantment, however, Longchenpa begins each chapter of analogy with recollection of the atiyoga recognition of our present situation in duplicitous samsara thereby opening up the reality of the nondual. Here in maya yoga with the realization that nonduality is the natural state of being, form and emptiness are seen as inseparable.

The term maha-ati denotes involuntary recognition of the nature of mind in every moment of experience. Atiyoga is the last resort in the relative world before conviction in the reality of the natural state of being brings about its own intrinsic nondual actuality. It is here that the radical Dzogchen view and nonmeditation engage. This is where the yogas of Cutting Through (trekcho) and Direct Crossing (togel), taken as a lifestyle, optimize confidence in maha-ati. The outer and inner *ruzhen* practises, the vocalization of the syllable PHAT, for example, provide a powerful mode of deconstruction of intellectual interference in direct perception. When the Dzogchen view has been lost, the *semdzins* constitute a vital backup. They can provide subtle perceptual touchstones that re-open windows upon—and then doors back into—the Dzogchen view. Without contesting the precept that maha-ati cannot be achieved through any cause or condition, here we can practice maya yoga, actualising Longchenpa's profound instruction in *Finding Comfort and Ease in Enchantment*.

Instruction for the main practice given at the beginning of the meditation section in each of the eight chapters of analogy is essentially the same. It reiterates the crucial injunction 'Regard all experience as maya'. The instruction applies primarily to sitting meditation sessions, but insofar as it is also applicable in a moment-to-moment twenty-four hour a day meditation the instruction obviously cannot be interpreted as a directive to discursively analyse in ontological and phenomenological terms every sensory perception as it arises. Neither can it be the call for an intellectual discussion with ourself about the features of any particular perception or realization, although that should not be ruled out entirely. Rather, since every perception, objective or subjective, external or internal, is—in Longchenpa's oft repeated phrase—'absent yet apparent' the instruction provides a moment of pause, a space of non-referential samadhi, wherein the paradox of all situations, all perceptual and mental events, being nothing yet something, necessarily and immediately evoke the nature of mind, opening into the thought-free vast expanse wherein all experience is founded.

In this way the instruction 'Regard all experience as maya' may be taken as a perceptual touchstone and the practice could be classified as a semdzin of the third category, the category that facilitates release. Application of the precept, 'Regard all experience as a magic show', for example, immediately evokes the nature of mind and opens up the thought-free space wherein all experience is 'absent yet apparent'. By analogy, it is similar to the *vicara* in Ramana Mahashi's Advaita Vedanta, where the koan-like phrase 'Who am I?' serves to deracinate the intellect. Stymied by the insoluble dilemma of the paradox of an absent yet apparent ego, the mind must now relax into its own primordial nature. In Zen, koan practice serves that function.

In the main practice of maya yoga, sitting in silent meditation, an enduring tendency grows to advert again and again to the precept 'all experience is a magic show'. The resultant psychological dissonance is resolved only by surrender to the nature of mind. If at the outset the dissonance of that dilemma is felt only weakly, or if it diminishes through time, then some discursive elaboration may be used, like, 'This is all a dream; it's all floating in space without any foundation; there's nothing solid inside or outside; it's a conjuring trick of the intellect; it's all hallucination', and so on, and thereby a conceptual aspect of the Dzogchen view is re-established and the sense of a nondual all-inclusive supra-mental reality is entered upon. That discursive activity is curtailed as soon as even mere intuition of the truth presents itself. The experience of that intuition may at first be only momentary and we are returned again and again to the discursive mental function. Yet, since it is the intrinsic natural state of presence that we are intuiting, as we gain increasing familiarity with it, it becomes progressively easier. Longchenpa's eight analogies—dream, magical illusion, echo, apparition, etc.—serve as illustration of the 'always already' reality of the immediately cognisant experience of all events as maya, ever 'absent yet apparent'.

The European Reformation fed on the perennial mystic tendency to reject complex, structured religious consciousness, priestly intercession, time-consuming eschatological ritual and scholastic dogma and abstruse liturgy. The psychedelic movement of the 'sixties brought nondualism out of the closet until today in the 'new age' there is a cognitive bias toward a formlessness of religious perspective reminiscent of the Dzogchen view. We take satisfaction, for instance, in the self-dissolving precepts of that view, precepts that interrupt the train of dogmatic discursive thought and with it, incidentally, the habit of obsessive/compulsive fundamentalist thinking so hated by the humanists. Just as the humanistic ethos that structures and determines the cognitive and moral imperatives of contemporary western culture was distilled from traditional Christian culture, so Dzogchen supersedes ritualistic, gradualist, Tibetan Tantra. But like most religious traditions Tibetan tantric Buddhism is part and parcel of the culture that spawned it. So it is with the Nyingma School's Longchen Nyingtik tradition, for example, which is embedded in the Tibetan monastic and priestly Buddhist tradition, inseparable from the sophisticated religious ritual and cultural forms and lifestyles of theocratic Tibet; yet the radical nondual precepts that are at its very heart demand its own existential—cognitive and syntactical—deconstruction and its own transcendence. Thus we move toward a realization that the religious context is irrelevant to the essential Dzogchen quest. Why, then, should we in the Western tradition replace our home-grown variety of religious forms with Central Asian paradigms? Certainly Tibetan Buddhism is in a state of rapid transition and growth in the West and the assimilation of esoteric Buddhism with its far-reaching multifaceted and profound metaphysical, psychological and moral implications will continue to serve and enrich western culture and benefit its people. But the Dzogchen view presupposes no specific religious-cultural base. Atiyoga precepts may be applied in any social milieu whatsoever and it is that feature that makes it—and its maya yoga—so eminently importable into western societies.

This is not true of mahayoga, however. Mahayoga is characterized as the creative process of meditation where ritual visualization of the symbolic forms of buddha-deities and the recitation of their mantras is believed to purify the karma of the meditator and also, at the ritual's conclusion, allow the clear light of the Great Perfection to arise. The foundational practice that Longchenpa introduces at the beginning of the first section on meditation, in *Dream: The First Analogy*, is a mahayoga exercise consisting primarily of 'creative' visualization and also a 'fulfilment' stage element of tantric practice. The antidote to the false dilemma posed by the intrusion of this non-formless element of meditation into the atiyoga scenario is the Dzogchen view in which relative and absolute are inseparable and where space/time is subsumed by nonduality. Here we are required to accept the small ritual of guru-yoga that through its symbolic structure and content reflects the actuality here and now of the Great Perfection. The inexpressible nondual Dzogchen view is not to be replaced by the psychology of the gradual path in which a conditioned belief system promotes a series of goals to be achieved through time wherein goal-orientation inevitably obsesses us. We should not fall into the error of conceiving that the mind-set implied by *Finding Comfort and Ease in Enchantment* rests upon the foundation that has been cultivated by the two preceding volumes of Longchenpa's trilogy. We should not err in believing that the actualization of the principal precepts of maya yoga rest upon the foundation of dream meditation. We may realize, however, that the creative and fulfilment forms of mahayoga provide moments of unfoldment through immediate intuitive understanding of their nature that spontaneously illuminate our clouded state of dualistic perception. We fall into the deep well of goal-obsession if we believe that contrived meditation through time will purify conventional maya; if on the other hand the magic of interactive visualized and conceptual symbols in mahayoga give us recognition and then familiarization with the nature of mind, this guru-yoga opens the way into the matrix of the timeless moment of pure presence.

If that explanation—or justification—still evokes the psychology of the gradual path, it may be useful to recall the traditional metaphor of the king at the centre of his court. Just as a king calls upon his minsters to provide expertise and ministerial functions according to their skills and aptitudes to facilitate his projects and purposes, so the Dzogchen yogi or yogini at the centre of the mandala spontaneously includes any of the vast array of skilful means and practices arranged as in concentric circles at varying proximity to him, according to their relevance, in completing the timeless moment of pure presence. 'The king's employment of his ministers' in the Dzogchen mandala of praxis is exemplified by Longchenpa's encouragement to practise the methods that the tradition offers to deconstruct emotion (at the end of the last stanza of *The City of the Gandharvas: The Seventh Analogy*). This instruction can be understood as practice of the semdzin wherein emotion is allowed to arise under our gaze only to dissolve immediately into its evanescence as the nature of mind. In that case we remain in the arena of atiyoga. If emotions are intractable and our gaze is weak we may utilize the similar tantric precepts that transform the five emotions into the five aspects of primal awareness represented by the five buddhas. Or perhaps we engage the bodhisattva vow and the six perfections that are specific antidotes to emotional states, like the perfection of patience as an antidote to anger (at the end of *Echo: The Sixth Analogy*). In these latter cases, although we may include in atiyoga whatever skilful means the lower eight approaches provide to deal with difficult karmically induced propensities, Dzogchen atiyoga is sustained in awareness of the all-inclusive nondual nature of mind that resolves the relative/absolute intellectual dualism.

Returning, however, to the ritual meditation of guru-yoga, it is comprised of visualization of the Guru and then relaxation into the clear light at dissolution of the visualization. This eight-line guru-yoga as the central, foundational practice may seem a small matter to spend such length of discussion upon, yet it is of crucial importance. The meditation of maya yoga—particularly of the waking state and dream yoga—is realized only insofar as guru-yoga is accomplished therein. All the precepts of atiyoga are mere nominal constructions unless the reality that the guru represents in our visualization, and which guru-yoga induces, is the reality of our dharma. In *Apparition: The Eighth Analogy*, where Longchenpa rehearses the cognitive Dzogchen dialectic of all the previous analogies, in his final phase of existential deconstruction wherein even those precepts that denominate the technical illusion of maya are denied validity insofar as they are intellectually determined constructs, he provides the ultimate Dzogchen precept: only the guru's blessing can facilitate the recognition that constitutes a breaking through into the nature of mind.

Guru-yoga develops our sense of the Guru from a venerable mentor, an embodied teacher existing 'outside' with which we have a relationship of subservience, to an internal voice or touchstone to whom we relate as a brother, and finally to the nondual reality that is the nature of mind. This reality is represented by Guru Rinpoche, Pema Jungney, the Great Guru whose emanation constitutes all our experience. His body is the form of the universe in any given moment; his voice is all sound and all vibration; his mind is the one mind of primal awareness. The guru's blessing, therefore, is a timeless adventitious moment totally free of personality and relationship. Adventitious, constantly available, this blessing is free of linear causes and rational conditioning, so that any strategy or agenda to contrive it is futile.

Longchenpa expresses the inexpressible pure presence, the gnosis (*rigpa*), that is the nature of the guru's blessing, through the analogy of apparition, all couched in his sublime, inimitable, poetry. If the guru's blessing is an opening of the inner eye of wisdom, then all colour and form and all sound and vibration, all energy formations, provide the effulgence of the nature of mind. A word of warning (in the penultimate verse of *Apparition: The Eighth Analogy*): railing against the scholars, pundits and monks who are caught up in the logic of their habitual conceptual beliefs and belief systems and whose thoughts are understood by themselves and others to be authoritatively incontrovertible, thereby inhibiting natural radiance shining through, Longchenpa defines the ignorance that precludes the guru's blessing. The blessing, he implies, is suffused with humility.

In the lines of the colophon, Longchenpa identifies himself as Stainless Radiance (Drimey Wozer), 'the yogi attending closely at the feet of the Great Guru Pema Jungney'. Here, surely 'the Great Guru Pema' is a poetic name for the immaculate maya of mind's nature, the name that evokes the famous image of Guru Rinpoche reclining upon the pristine lotus, representing the dynamic nature of mind arising spontaneously out of the mud of the lake of endless samsara, experienced in the nonspecific form of the buddhas' trikaya. Here, at the end of his composition Longchenpa reveals that he has never been far away from guru-devotion. Nothing but devotion to that Guru allows entry into the throes of the inspired composition displayed in his work. Nothing but relaxation into the nature of mind and unity with it provides the knowledge in which the Dzogchen precepts can be woven. This 'weaving of the Dzogchen precepts in pure presence' is a fine metaphor in the context of radical Dzogchen, at the conclusion of a work on maya where spaciousness (*dharmadhatu*) is a synonym of maya.

In the timeless moment of the guru's blessing the four samayas of Dzogchen atiyoga—absence, openness, spontaneity and oneness—are recognized as binding us primordially, involuntarily, whether we know it or not. Throughout his recollection of the precepts of both view and meditation, Longchenpa articulates the key words that evoke and affirm these samayas. In particular, maya is 'absent', its absence indicated in every use of the phrase 'absent yet apparent' that constantly points at the paradoxical nondual. With realisation of the meaning of this crucial phrase in maya yoga the tendency to nihilism at worst, and the samadhi of nothingness at best—both of which contemplation of absence may unwittingly encourage—are uprooted. Maya is absent insofar as it lacks any substantiality as an ego, a soul or a 'Self'. It is non-existent, and likewise untrue and unreal. Yet it is still sensate, apparent, visible. The force of contemplation upon absence is to nullify our inveterate propensity to conceive of substance in our perception of the external world and to 'feel' a separate individuality, a sense of self, in our inner lives and personality. Ego-loss is contingent upon recognition of this absence.

The second of the Dzogchen samayas, openness, is evoked by its synonyms, particularly 'emptiness' (*sunyata*) which Longchenpa employs frequently, usage unusual in a Dzogchen context. Emptiness may imply an absence of any conceptual attribute whatsoever, but in its implication and connotation of open-ended light-form the term 'openness' has been used by some translators as an equivalent of *sunyata* (most prominently by Dr Guenther). Further, wherever, the nature of mind in its vast spaciousness is evoked by Longchenpa's simile of the sky, which is frequent, openness as emptiness is to be inferred.

The first pair of samayas—absence and openness—apply to the phase of Cutting Through and the second pair—spontaneity and oneness—to Direct Crossing, the phase of fruition. In a text that deals with the practical application of the precepts of Cutting Through, the second pair appears less frequently. Spontaneity and oneness refer to the place where intellectually conceived constructs no longer apply, where karmically induced conditioning has lost its force.

The Eight Analogies

The text is divided into eight chapters, each treating one of the eight analogies, the whole concluding with verses of dedication. Each chapter is divided into sections of View and Meditation. The divisions in the sections of View and Meditation are indicated in the translation by extra interlinear spaces.

The section on view in each of the eight chapters of analogy begins with a reminder of the nondual reality of the clear light of the nature of mind (the natural state of being) in which the delusory condition of our ordinary samsaric experience arises. The former is called basic immaculate magical illusion and the latter the magical illusion of false concepts. That distinction is elaborated at the beginning of *Dream*, where Longchenpa introduces it as the starting point of his treatise—we begin by recognizing our prison of dualistic constructs. Here, also, in his description of our delusory vision he makes the distinction between the loss of awareness that arises adventitiously, simultaneously, with every sensory perception and the loss of awareness that accompanies the intellectual ideational and conceptual activity of selecting, filtering and projecting the concepts that we then take as conventional illusion. Each chapter likens our experience of the magical illusion of false concepts to one of the eight analogies—dream, magic show, mirage, echo, etc.

The distinction between the immaculate maya that is our natural state of being and the maya polluted by intellectual activity is emphasized in order that recognition of the latter as nothing other than the former may resolve the ostensible dualism between our natural state of being and our present state of ignorance. That distinction is introduced here as the basis of the understanding of the need 'to chill out behind enchantment'. This is the skilful means of atiyoga and allows the Dzogchen dialectic to perform its magic, beginning with the assertion that since ignorance arises in and as the pristine nature of mind, it never becomes anything other than the nature of mind. The illusion that it does become a separate reality is indicated by the diaphanous delusiveness of the eight analogies. The remainder of the sections on view in *Dream* provides an understanding of how the delusion that arises out of the immaculate natural state of being is like experience of the respective analogy, all couched in precepts employing the imperative mood of the verb—'recognize', 'realize', 'see', etc. The final lines in each section on view return to an assertion of nonduality.

The section on meditation in each chapter treats first the yoga of the waking state and then dream yoga. Instruction on the foundational practices and the guru-yoga that are prescribed in all of the eight aspects of the waking aspect of maya yoga are given at the beginning of the Meditation section in *Dream*. After these preliminaries, in each of the eight meditations we are instructed to aspire to maya-consciousness by evoking the actual nature of the relevant analogy. This aspiration is couched in the verbal form of prayer. 'May I recognize all my experience as dream,' for example. It asserts the implication that the insight of the view is inseparable from the praxis of the meditation. Since view and meditation are two sides of the same existential coin, this is axiomatic in Dzogchen. This principle may be inferred here from the lack of any substantial difference in the nature of the preceptual instruction in the sections on view and of waking meditation (and also perhaps in dream-yoga). What is the difference experientially, for example, between the imperative to 'recognize spontaneous self-existent intrinsic presence' and the instruction 'to let our minds settle, without fluctuation, without hope or fear in the mirage-like space of all experience (*The Fourth Analogy*)' or 'to settle in sameness, allowing the mind to perceive whatever arises like the reflection of the moon in water' (*The Fifth Analogy*).

Further, it becomes evident here that the main praxis of this maya yoga is identical in all eight aspects. The distinction lies only in the doorway that we use to enter the same room. The discursive thought with which we begin the reinforcement of the insight that all experience is like a dream, for example, or that this particular moment of experience is like a dream, is a gateway into the same recognition of all maya as immaculate. The practice of dream yoga is described at length in the first analogy—*Dream*—and in a shorter exposition in the second analogy—*Magic Show*. It is only mentioned in passing in the subsequent chapters because, again, the practice remains essentially the same. Longchenpa's purpose is that each of the eight analogies provides fresh insight into the nature of reality (*dharma*), into all our experience (*dharma*), every event and situation (*dharma*), as maya. The following synopses include salient features selected from Longchenpa's intense and dense literary style.

Dream: The First Analogy

The first chapter presents the view, meditation and fruit of maya yoga. The short section on View introduces the basic notion of maya as twofold, immaculate maya and conceptualized maya, and then differentiates intrinsic loss of awareness and the ignorance of intellectual constructs and concepts. The precepts of view assert the unitary nature of twofold maya as the sky-like awareness that is like dream. The long section on meditation describes the meditations that actualize the insight of the view. Each session of meditation begins with the foundation of refuge and bodhi-mind and then guru-yoga. The main praxis initiated during the session of meditation and thereafter reinforced during every meditation session is the dream-yoga that is the moment-to-moment, twenty-four/seven, nonmeditation that we experience in the breaks between formal meditation sessions

This dream-yoga has two parts: waking dream and sleeping dream. In both the contemplation is the same.

Aware of the inherent insubstantiality of all appearances, all situations, waking or sleeping, we relax into the unreality of all experience, into the reality of nondual maya. In sleep, through an absence of attachment to dream, we dream lucid dream. Here transformation and multiplication of emanation, and travel in the dream world, provide a paradigm that fulfils the purposes of compassionate pure presence. The chapter ends with a brief indication not only of the creativity that is engendered by sleeping dream-yoga, but also of the product of the twenty-four/seven nonmeditation practice.

Magic Show: The Second Analogy

It should be noted that 'magic show' can have two meanings according to where the stress is laid in the phrase. A *magic* show is a conjuror's professional gig. A magic *show* is a magical display, in our case a multi-dimensional, omni-sensory, display of maya. The former is an analogy or simile of maya; the latter is a metaphorical description of it. The simile of the conjuror's or illusionist's performance is the analogy of *magic* show that runs through this chapter, wherein Longchenpa introduces the four instances of maya that are germane to maya yoga: the maya of our everyday lives that is the real nature of mind, yet still deceives us; maya as the deception perceived as something to be decontaminated; maya as sadhana—the praxis of decontamination; and maya as the pristine phantasmagoria of intrinsic awareness.

To illustrate that all our samsaric perceptions are the tortuous elaborations of simplicity like a conjuror's illusion that appears as more than its constituent props, Longchenpa evokes our perception of other minds, other people. Like oneself, other people have no intrinsic substantial nature and therefore cannot be said to exist independently as a constant or even as a flash of light. We know them only as our projections intellectually larded with deep ingrained constructs and ephemeral yet habitual assumptions about them, all of which determine their perceived attributes and personalities. People are nothing more than phantasms, like those that populate our daydreams.

To reinforce the notion of the duplicity of maya, we can say that our perception of people is a lie and that our perception of the world we live in is a universal lie. Because the recognition of those lies provide an occasion for lightness of being we can also call it a joke—a cosmic joke. Longchenpa insinuates the notion of the universal lie and the cosmic joke into the section on meditation.

Optical Illusion: The Third Analogy

The distinction should be clarified between optical illusion and hallucination. An optical illusion is derived from a visual hook that is interpreted falsely by the eye and intellect, like a black piece of cloth hanging in the rafters that is taken for a bat. Alternatively, the visual hook may become the occasion for an elaborate fantasy, like a movement of light and shadow that appears to be a scampering rat, or the milder fantasies of *delirium tremens* where wallpaper patterns appear to be invasive spiders. An hallucination is a mental projection independent of any exterior handle. It is traditionally illustrated by the compelling delusions induced by the psychotropic plant *dhatora* (thorn apple).

Hallucination could also serve as a simile of maya but Longchenpa deals here in the third analogy with optical illusion in order to undermine our belief in an apparently concrete external world. The emphasis here is on the external world as delusion because it has no core, no nuclear essence or 'self'. Our samsaric environment is certainly visible to the senses but it is actually non-existent, 'absent', because it is groundless. Examine it with the eye of insight and like optical illusion it vanishes and our rational reservations inevitably disperse. The seemingly external sensory panorama appears to be real only because of our need to perceive cognitive security in every sensory event, a process that flows naturally from our emotional validation of an ego or self in order to be free of the fear of ego-loss. Thus, recognition of the sky-like nature of mind is directly proportional to our ego-loss.

Mirage: The Fourth Analogy

In his perusal of mirage Longchenpa discovers the best illustration of maya as absent yet apparent, non-existent but visible. However, just as the rational mind stumbles and halts, spaced out, in the perception of paradoxical mirage, so looking into polluted maya as fictional delusion the mind is returned to its nondual unoriginated state. The totality-vision of polluted maya, seemingly substantial, rests upon the sense of an ego and since nothing of that kind exists as we gaze into the nature of mind, the intellect is confounded and the natural state of nirvana is revealed.

The Reflection of the Moon in Water: The Fifth Analogy

Maya is *like* the reflection of the moon in water, or *like* a reflection in a mirror. Maya is *not* a reflection of a discrete, separately existent, object. In another famous analogy evoked in atiyoga the sensory phantasmagoria is likened to the rainbow spectrum produced by the refraction of a sunbeam through a crystal. Maya may be a *refraction* of clear light, but it is not a *reflection* of a seemingly concrete object. The significance of the reflection of the moon in water, again, is its magical nature. It appears but has no substantial existence. We cannot put a finger upon it, let alone grasp it. Try to touch an image of the moon in water and the clear reflection disperses into dazzling proliferation of ripples. We simply need to recognize it as it is.

Within the sublime calm and pristine primal awareness that is evoked by the image of the yogin sitting by a still pool of water on a full moon night contemplating the moon's reflection, Longchenpa, in his fifth analogy, moves along to introduce the notion of spontaneity and to reinforce the precept of non-action. In this Dzogchen context the word 'spontaneity' does not describe so much the manner of appearance of an image in the pellucid nature of mind but rather characterizes the image itself. The image is not so much 'spontaneously created', implying a creator, a creation and the act of creating, but rather it is a timeless moment of inexpressible reality neither created in a temporal process nor existing as a crystallized object of creation. The maya of all situations is spontaneity, free of the limitations of all temporal concepts. Non-action, on the other hand, is the natural state of mind in which the spontaneity occurs, implying surrender of all goal-orientation and seeking strategies. Wherever we are exhorted to just let it be and relax into the nature of mind, into unitary space, into the natural state of being, non-action is indicated. Non-action, however, does not necessarily imply inaction, passivity or stasis; it entails neither a loss or diminution of efflorescence nor any particular manner of being.

Echo: The Sixth Analogy

In the Dzogchen view Longchenpa employs the analogy of echo to evoke the nature of mind in all experience, in every event. It is not so much aural perception that is treated here but rather the similarity of echo to every sensory experience in that it is devoid of substance, and empty, having no evident source, seemingly without cause. With this recognition there is nothing further to do. There is no distinction to be made between absolute and relative because experience of the moment is beyond the intellect and nothing we may think or believe makes any difference to the reality of immaculate maya.

In the section on meditation, after exhorting us to recognize all experience to be empty like echo, Longchenpa focuses on the emptiness of all sound. Especially, he considers the emptiness of words of praise and blame in order to illustrate the emptiness of all sensory impressions whatsoever. When taking other people's words as the occasion for familiarising ourselves with all experience as echo, besides realizing the nature of mind we cultivate the invaluable virtue of patience. Likewise, looking with insight into burgeoning emotion, particularly anger, taking it as an adventitious circumstance, like echo, cultivating the experience of all phenomena as echo, we are relieved of the conditions that produce neurotic emotional states.

The City of the Gandharvas: The Seventh Analogy

The city of the gandharvas is a land of myth, like Fairie, or Jerusalem the Golden. Like Udyana (where Padma Sambhava was born) or Hollywood, it has a geographical location, but geography is relevant here only insofar as it gives the vision of that city greater credibility. Like Jerusalem the Golden, the city of the gandharvas is an externalized vision in the sky. As an internal vision it is a daydream or pipe dream; externally it is castles in the air, cloudland or cloud cuckoo land. In Buddhist mythology the gandharvas who populate it are celestial musicians, but again that is only tangentially relevant here.

In this seventh analogy Longchenpa goes further in his identity of polluted maya and immaculate maya. He states in so many words that the nature of samsara is nirvana. We need only recognize our sensorially designated world as space-based and we relax into the nondual primal awareness of the natural state of being.

At the end of the section on view Longchenpa prescribes a meditation for moments (and rebirths) when we fail to recognize the nature of mind in every instant of the here and now. We know intellectually that all experience is like a city of the gandharvas, a project of maya, that action is non-action in its essential nature, and that renunciation and engaged commitment are equally delusory. But while there is a vestigial belief in a real person or an ego, a cosmic substance or a god, so long as that recognition does not kick-in existentially the ego is left with a yearning for an unrealized ideal. In that case the recommendation is to work with the emotions, according to the precepts of Mahayana, Tantra or Dzogchen.

Apparition: The Eighth Analogy.

Longchenpa would have assumed that his audience was familiar in their own lives with apparitions, whether they were ghosts of departed souls, visitations of local spirits and gods, or visions of buddha-deities and so on. Such apparitional vision was part of the religious culture of Tibet. Our western materialistic culture tends at best to discourage such experience and at worst to ridicule it. So the first lesson to be drawn from *Apparition* is tolerance, acceptance and finally surrender to the phenomena of apparition itself. This approach to maya as apparition is useful because by envisioning ghosts, for example, the rational mind is stymied, boggled, and naturally retreats into abeyance, allowing the nature of mind to shine through.

In this extensive eighth chapter Longchenpa rehearses the entire Dzogchen view of the seven previous chapters. But as a culmination of his moving focus from the external world that he treats as the primary consideration in the early chapters it is the living beings on the wheel of life that he defines firstly by reference to apparition. The living beings, however, inseparable from their environments, are coalesced into a unitary illusion that is like an apparition. The totality of this vast illusion, including its emotional content, when left alone, free of intellectual interference, is none other than the reality of our buddha-nature, expressed as the buddha-trikaya and buddha-fields, boundless openness, pure and pristine—the nature of mind.

With the experientially based conviction that the entire mandala of our experience is like an apparition, we can burn our progressivist bridges and slowly abandon the process of egoic intellectual deconstruction that has brought us to this point. The dualism of subject and object that particularizes and concretizes specific elements of our experience is no longer valid, so like rabbits' horns all our fictive imputations upon the emptiness of reality dissolve. Our opinions and preferences become a part of the universal, intersubjective, delusion and the only reality is what lies beyond ideational concepts and constructs, and the interpretive and selective functions of cognitive mind. No verbal formulation whatsoever can do justice to experience after it is recognized as apparitional light-form. Labels are for the birds. Any discussion about the nature of reality is mere speculative hot air. Even the verbal function of pointing out the nature of mind is delusion.

FINDING COMFORT AND EASE IN ENCHANTMENT

Homage to Vajrasattva!
In the space where all experience remains in potential,
emerges a grand display of nondual awareness and illusion,
the original spontaneity of our sovereign nature of mind:
indivisible from that, unmoving, to that we bow down.

Dream: The First Analogy

To understand what the buddhas mean in their impeccable revelation
that all our experience has two dimensions of magical illusion,
I have distilled here the elixir of sutra, tantra and oral instruction.
Listen while I impart it to you in the light of my personal
experience.

In unchanging basic spaciousness, the vast sky of mind's nature,
a space of unstructured brilliance and emptiness,
flawless buddha-reality shines like the stars
as the spontaneity of inseparable being and awareness.*
This intrinsic clear light, with its perfect responsive spontaneity,
this is our original, natural state of being,
known as basic immaculate magical illusion.

But in that very space, pure presence is lost,
clouds of delusion arising adventitiously,
for ignorance, like sleep, is a dream-maker.
The spoiled mind, mistaking unity for duality,
in its loss of pure presence spawns the universal delusion,
the six mythic modes of being† in their environments.
Just like dream, they are seemingly real but without existence,
and we feel the misery or the joy of each of them.

From time immemorial, conditioned to such relativity,
our environment, corporeality, pleasures—our lives,
envisioned as good or bad, are happy or sad;

---

* Being (*kaya*) is the *trikaya*, the three-dimensional buddha-reality (*dharmakaya*, *sambhogakaya* and *nirmanakaya*), and awareness (*jnana*) is the unitary field of holistic primal awareness.

† Gods, demons, men, animals, hungry ghosts and hell beings.

out of delusion, unity appears in manifold guises,
like an infinite variety of realistic graphic art,
and, believing in them, delusive appearances are incessant.
Ah, yes, this world is just a dream.

This dualizing intellect's multifarious dream world,
the delusive appearances of an ignorant sleep,
aroused in the unitary essence that is the nature of mind—
and therefore nothing other than the nature of mind—
this the buddhas call the magical illusion of false conception.

Just as under the influence of dhatura
when our hallucinations seem so real,
be sure, here and now, that in this sleep of ignorance,
our visible projections, the six mythic modes of being,
are all fiction, as if we were hallucinating.

This delusory world hangs upon our delusive clinging
and delusive intellectual constructs.
But cherishing the nonduality of true and false,
beyond the intellect,
we recognize the spontaneity of self-sprung intrinsic presence,
and in that vast matrix where 'is' and 'is not' implode
we recognize the sky-like buddha-dynamic.

The actuality of all experience is like a dream
and in its momentary groundless gleaming,
undeniably perceptible, it is uncrystallizing light-form,
a deceitful flash, a diaphanous form of emptiness.
Yet delving deeply we find neither truth nor falsehood,
for neither present nor absent, it is beyond all conception;
we know it like the sky, inexpressible, unimaginable,
fundamentally ever fresh and pristine.

The Meditation

Utterly convinced of this view that all situations,
samsara and nirvana, are just like dream,
follow this instruction to experience it in meditation.

Sit upon a comfortable seat in half-lotus posture,
take triple-gem refuge and cultivate pure bodhi-mind,
then in empty unitary space,
which is the utter sameness of all experience,
apply concentrated attention to this empty magic spell.

On the crown of the head, upon a lotus, sun and moon throne
clearly envision the root guru, embodying yidam and dakini,
inseparable from the lineage gurus.
Worship and praise him, aspiring to cultivate a sense of dream,
then allowing oneself and environment to dissolve into light,
which then vanishes into the guru,
hang loosely for a moment in sky-like space.
The blessings of realization rain down by themselves.

Then as the main praxis meditate like this:
The outer world, its mountains and valleys,
villages and towns and its living beings,
compounds of earth, water, fire, air and space,
all forms, sounds, smells, tastes and sensations,
the five sensory objects,
and the internal world of body-mind
and its sensory consciousness,
all experience, should be attended to incessantly as dream.

All of our life's experiences up to yesterday,
just mental images, are like last night's dream,

and what we see now, absent yet crystal clear,
absent yet apparent, is the mind's delusion.
Yesterday and today are just like dream;
tomorrow and the day after, all our future, only dream.

Fully conditioned to the idea that everything is dream,
whether it is affirmed or denied, pleasant or painful,
do not think for a moment that the mind is true.
Moving or sitting, eating, walking or talking,
with constant attention sustain dream-consciousness.
When all that we see, all that we do, all that we think,
is consonant with dream, our experience is disassociated,
unfocussed, in slow motion, evanescent.
That is training in ultimate non-attachment.

Appreciating delusory objective appearances as dream,
the intellect lets go and the grasping immediately ceases—
the objective aspect debunked, the subjective side retires.
Then whenever the mind meets situations as dream,
the intellect searching inside and outside and in between
for something substantial and solid to grasp,
unable to find any point of reference
it subsides into all-penetrating sky-like space,
and intrinsic presence devoid of all compulsive mental activity
arises spontaneously as simple empty clarity.

Grasping ceasing, nothing to be grasped,
the vessel inverted, its contents lost,
phenomena are disassociated, lacking any boundaries.
That is nondual unconditional primal awareness.

Upon complete familiarity with that realization,
by involuntary resolution of the duality of grasper and grasped,
we are free of the compulsive attraction of mind to an object,
and with a definite feeling of detachment from situations,
whatever presents itself, timeless, empty, floats in space.
That is the natural primordial state of being.

Once its credibility has thus been lost,
enslavement to impure circumstantial illusion
becomes dominant pure enchantment.
As if we were never to awaken from lucid dream,
pure mind infuses the primordial ground.

Each delusion, without past or future but shining in between,
envisioned in the here and now, is not felt as existent;
the intellect's karma-induced delusion, absent yet visible,
since its nature is primordially pure, is like dream.

Just as we know dream as internal vision,
absent before sleeping and after waking,
shining only during sleep, and even then without substance,
just so we should know phenomena as groundless and baseless.

While in the daytime becoming familiar with dream-reality,
at night when the need to sleep overcomes us
we lie down on our right side upon a comfortable bed
like Buddha Sakyamuni in his nirvana posture.
When the breath is quiet and the eyes are still,
at the heart centre, with dreamlike concentration,
visualize a white A of shining bright translucent crystal,
diminishing in size from a finger tip to a hair tip,
and dreamlike clear light arises.

At first we may dream many fearful dreams,
but mindful of the dream the fear dissolves of itself;
when natural concentration is effortlessly achieved
the yogin knows his dream as lucid dream.

Thereafter the sole practice is to see all dream as unreal.
The absent but apparent delusory mind,
like dream, has no essence to grasp,
and we know it beyond intellectual truth and falsehood.

Then, regarding the process of transforming emanation:
in dream-time, to transform the body into Brahma, for instance,
or to emanate as a buddha or bodhisattva,
we simply relax with our wish into ambivalent space.

Like that, from moment to moment—
from Brahma to Indra, from god to man—
whatever transformation we desire
is accomplished in an unreal world.

Furthermore, now multiplying those forms
a hundred, a thousand, or ten million-fold,
we develop the facility to heal wherever needed.

Further, we travel wherever we wish,
to pure lands, to foreign countries, or to Akanishta*
where we see buddhas and hear their impeccable word
and achieve *jnana* and *samadhi* and multitudes of *dakinis*.†
Through thorough integrated practice day and night,

---

* Akanishta is the highest buddhafield.

† *Jnana* is nondual wisdom, *samadhi* is contemplation and *dakini* is pure vision

the creativity of pure presence will surely manifest,
the core undistorted, infallibly actualized:
that is the most profound way of the heart.

Day and night, familiarising ourselves with the dream world,
the shackles of belief in concrete materiality are shaken off;
enclosures, mountains and walls now form no impediment
and miracles, psychic powers and samadhis are actualized.

With deep experience of this direct and naked realization,
primal awareness, empty and luminous, dawns
and in the primordial spaciousness of the nature of mind
both subjective *dharmakaya*, and objective *rupakaya*,*
are spontaneously accomplished as in a dream.
Apply concentrated attention to the dream-mode!

---

* *Dharmakaya* is the holistic formless dimension of light and awareness and *rupakaya* is the dimension of formal emanation.

Magic Show: The Second Analogy

Again, the buddhas in their wisdom have said
that in their hollow insubstantiality
all situations are like a magic show.
Again, listen as I relate my personal experience
according to the heart-meaning of the crucial sutras,
the tantras and oral instruction.

Just as primal awareness spontaneously arises
in the sky-like space of the primordial nature of mind,
shining like luminous stellar spheres,
so, out of miraculous, all-penetrating, womblike spaciousness,
the imaginings of dualizing ignorance arise by themselves
as the delusory triple world
with its six mythic modes of being,*
which—absent yet apparent—is all magical show.

Through concatenating circumstances,
synchronistically, the magic show presents itself,
like horses and elephants, men and women,
mountains and palaces, and so on, conjured by a magician
using props of wood and stone and applying magic spells.

The potent ignorance of karmically conditioned delusory
intellect
displays our objective world of appearances and possibilities
where the three poisons,† subjectively, react to it,
and we realize, unequivocally, in this very moment,

---

* The sky, the earth and the subterranean worlds populated by humans, gods, demons, animals, ghosts and devils.

† Desire, anger and sloth.

that appearances, lacking any substance, never crystallizing,
with apparitional beings, the entirety of it,
comprise a marvellous seductive magical show of emptiness.

We recognize that all situations, samsara and nirvana,
fundamentally, are identical to the sky,
pure in their primordial unbegun beginning.

In that space of uncreated magical creation
the actual show that is the basis of transformation,
the polluted show that is to be disinfected,
the technical show of skilful decontamination,
and the ultimate show of primal awareness—
these four are mere instances of magic show.

In an illusionist's trick created by magic spells,
just as the wood and stone that appear as elephants and horses
are not elephants and horses but remain wood and stone,
so all situations, their unreality indicated,
must be seen as mere instances of magic show.

Basic delusion, its circumstances that are the delusory process,
the delusory release from those delusive appearances,
and the dynamic of primordial liberation
are indicated here as the four instances of magic show:
the introductory image illustrating the actuality of illusion,
the illustrative images of pollution and then decontamination,
and the illustrative image of the resultant state.

The actuality of the magic show is the clear light of mind's nature;
it is its spaciousness and it is the buddha-nature.
Undivided in terms of purity or impurity

since it lies beyond samsara and nirvana,
it is the spaciousness from which samsara and nirvana emerge;
it is the ground in which samsara or nirvana arises
according to the presence or absence of intrinsic presence;
it is our primordial essence; it is the natural state of our being.
This ground of being is like a bright mirror reflecting images
yet remaining untouched by the reflection of any image;
its surface containing neither black nor white colour
yet it is the fount of both black and white images.
With that understanding one may become wise.

The contaminated illusion is delusory samsaric appearance
arising in the ground due to the grasping of its unity as duality.

The technical illusion constitutes the cleansing process:
the fourfold 'preparing', 'applying', 'seeing' and 'familiarising'
mature the two accumulations and the two stages,*
removing the pollution of ignorance as clouds dissolve in the sky.

The culmination of the magic show of primal awareness
occurs in the phase of no-more-learning,
where the buddha-trikaya becomes active spontaneity,
and both essential purity and manifest purity are revealed.

All instances of magic show are synchronicitous magic
and like a magic show contrived from symbols and spells
all experience is exposed as insubstantial and unreal,
a small part of a web of continuously mutating illusion.

---

* The progressive accumulation of both skilful means and insight into all experience as emptiness are the two accumulations; and creative and fulfilment stages are the two aspects of mahayoga.

Thus we may realize the delusory nature of every perception
that looms larger than the bare bones of its constituent parts.

Consider, for example, our habitual perceptions of others—
delusive perceptions that have no reality,
mere images of synchronicitous karmically conditioned
assumptions,
in this very moment, empty, insubstantial, ungraspable.
and we recognize them now to be beyond dualistic identity.

We now know the six mythic modes of being as delusions,
fantasy beings with fantasy pleasures,
fantasy feelings and fantasy lives and deaths,
believing in fantasy truths and falsehoods,
populating fantasy lands and fantasy cities,
.
Pure from the very beginning, it is all a magic show,
magic show because it is apparent but has no real existence,
magic show because it is a function of coincidental conditions,
magic show because it deceives and enchants then vanishes:
brand all samsaric appearances as delusory, as 'magic show'.

If we fail to realize what has been made patently obvious,
that the six mythic modes of being are but apparitional magic,
we wander unceasingly in this boundless city of samsara,
tortured by our karmically induced feelings—how sad!
Understand, beloved! Conventional appearances are fantasy!

You fortunate ones, convinced by your direct experience,
you recognize that no situation has any reality,
that emerging from nothing and vanishing into nothing,
pure from the beginning it is all but a magical show.

You recognize, you lucky ones,
that the nature of sentient beings is apparition,
the nature of pure mind is the spaciousness of illusion,
and nondual samsara-nirvana is the play of that illusion.

The buddha has said that his only message is enchantment:
we recognize, all of us who seek release,
that the duplicitous totality itself is enchanting reality.

Enchanting illusion can also be known like this:
it is a magic show of pure mind
that is immutable, unchanging, spontaneity;
it is a guileless ubiquitous master, like the sky,
like the sun, or like a wish-fulfilling gem,
displaying unlimited creativity and total responsiveness,
that is the unelaborated simplicity of pure radiance.

The magic show that is samsara, spurious and beguiling,
lacking any definition, is evanescent like phantom;
in the moment when delusive concepts leave it,
it dissolves into its own spaciousness.
Just as horses and elephants cease to appear
when the conjuror's spell is broken,
so tainted samsara's perceptual duality
resolves itself into its own primordial nature,
and now empty in its purity, it loses all identity.

The magic show of the natural state is immutable reality,
the reality that includes both polluted and pristine;
just as the internal space of both clay and golden vessels,
whether damaged or intact, neither increases nor decreases,
so in moments of both delusion and freedom
reality itself remains a nonjudgmental constant.
This is buddha-mind in its natural state of being
and knowing this one is truly wise.

The Meditation

Behind the realization of this view of magical illusion
we cultivate enchanting illusion as the cosmic joke.
In preparation, as before, aspire to a sense of magical illusion.

Constantly, day and night, moment by moment,
our main work is to attend to each inner and outer event
as magical show appearing by force of circumstance,
as lies, without heart or meaning, diaphanous and unreal.

Our loves and hatreds, positive and negative affectivity,
whatsoever emotions are aroused,
certify them as illusion. Train in this unreality.
We see now that both outer, seemingly material phenomena
and inner, mental experience, are all like magic show.
Because they are contrived by circumstance,
because they are spurious and duplicitous,
because they are mere light-form,
always regard them as instances of a magic show.

At time for sleep, as before, relax into dream-space,
into enchanted unreality, unelaborate in its simplicity.
Whatever delusive dreams arise are now known as illusion
and we are free from fear and craving for truth.
Working dream as illusion, transforming emanation,
travelling magically into pure lands, cultivate all as before.

Now the addiction to samsara bursts open
and freedom in illusion is unabiding nirvana,
the spontaneous achievement of our dual illusory purpose.*
Attend to this persistent reality that is nothing but illusion!

---

* Benefit for oneself and for others.

Optical Illusion: The Third Analogy

Again, the buddhas in their wisdom have said
that all our experience is like optical illusion.
Listen to my elucidation of that statement.

Just as optical illusion springs out of a colour or shape
so by the force of karmically induced delusion
the optical illusion of samsara, absent yet apparent,
dawns in the space of mind's nature—
here every situation appears like an optical illusion.

The unwise in their naïveté, craving truth, are beguiled,
lost in the jungle of fivefold sensory illusion.
Be aware of the error of fixating on something that is nothing!

The sensory world, environment and beings,
happy and sad feelings and mood-swings,
all absent yet perceptible, are like ominous shadows cast by
 a lamp,
like a double image appearing when the eyeball is pressed,
like projected fears on a dark night.
They exist only at face value, vanishing under examination,
while deep insight reveals their wide-open nature
that is uncreate, like the sky, timeless primordial reality.
We can see it in this moment, here and now!

Samsaric appearances, unfounded, are like optical illusion,
their very rootlessness undoing all defining features;
with insight, they appear as hollow, insubstantial light-form
and we recognize their primordially unoriginated nature.
Just as a small object in the middle of an empty plain,

although insignificant assumes vast importance,
so from a tendentious belief in empty self as solid ego
samsara's delusory panorama arises and materializes.

Under scrutiny that delusory vision dematerializes
and it is evident that like the sky it is impotent,
mere light-form without existence, like optical illusion,
so we just let it be, denying it all credibility.

It is pure space! it is timeless! it is primordially pristine!
Do not try to localize it! do not try to conceptualize it!
What is inchoate light without dimension
cannot be caged by obsessive, biased, constructs.

It is better to surrender all ideas about it
and recognize it all as devoid of truth.
So we recognize all events as optical illusion
and rest the weary mind, just as it is, in its primordial nature.

The Meditation

To prepare, as before, and aspire to see all things as optical illusion.
As the main praxis, gain familiarity with that insight.
See all colour and form as unreal, like optical illusion;
hear all sounds as empty, like figments of the ear,
all aromas, tastes, tactile sensations, as sensory figment,
all mental activity and internal experience as figments of mind.
Hang loosely in the space where everything is unreal,
free of the intellect's obsessive addictive beliefs.

As in the day so at nighttime: fix the mind in the heart centre
and sleep in the space where everything is like optical illusion.
Lucid dream, and so on, as before, will certainly arise.

Even visionary experiences and insights are like dream,
and instinctively recognizing that there is no truth anywhere,
in detached transparency both positive and negative
projections collapse.
The eye of insight, psychic powers, samadhis
and perfectly responsive spontaneity are achieved,
and now living as buddha we may provide guidance to all
living beings.
Familiarize yourselves with all situations as optical illusion!

Mirage: The Fourth Analogy

The buddhas in their wisdom have said
all experience is like mirage.
Listen now as I elucidate that truth.

Just as in the heat of a summer day
a mirage, a watered oasis, hovers over the desert plain,
so through the powerful habit of personifying mind as self
delusive mirage-like emanation appears in the mind-sky.

Without essence there to grasp as substantial,
in nature nondual, empty, the state of nirvana,
immaterial and self-less, like the sky, unbegun,
we know it as nonconceptual, unborn, beyond image and idea.

At the moment of its seeming appearance, whatever it is,
seemingly created yet unoriginated, it is like mirage;
seemingly existing yet unlocatable, it is like mirage;
seemingly concrete yet never crystallizing, it is like mirage:
see all appearances as intangible evanescence.

All moods, feelings and qualitative judgements,
like mirage, are mere vanity, empty in essence,
and the apparent world and our fictive lives,
all experience, inner and outer, all and everything,
like a mirage, does not exist but still shines,
its nature primordially ever-fresh and pristine.
We recognize it as timeless, without centre or parameter.

Even the duality of nondual light-form and emptiness is
 itself a mirage:
without compulsive assertion or denial of what is really frivolity

we see our dualized mind as nondual, merely a mirage:
here is our timeless ever-present buddha-mind.

The Meditation

Now regarding the meditative process of familiarization,
in preparation, do as before:
aspire to intuit all experience as mirage.
But the main point is to let the mind settle,
without fluctuation, without hope or fear,
in the mirage-like spaciousness of all experience.

At night, as before, we will feel the dream world as mirage.

Craving nothing, the ego losing itself,
magic spells, psychic powers, samadhis, issue from within,
and the buddha-state is quickly achieved.
Familiarize yourselves with actuality as a mirage!

Reflection of the Moon in Water: The Fifth Analogy

The buddhas in their wisdom have said
all experience is like the reflection of the moon in water
and here I explain it so you may realize it directly.

In the deep, pellucid lake of mind's nature
lie bright images of spontaneity, timelessly arisen;
but the rough polluting waves of dualistic perception
roils the clarity already churned by a storm of concepts.

That worldly confusion springs from belief in an ego, a self,
and primal awareness now opaque, dull and emotional,
sinks into beginningless and endless samsara.

Just as the stars' reflection in a pellucid pool of water
shines steadily, absent yet apparent,
so delusory images appear in the still mirror of mind,
and those evanescent images worry us.

Nothing solid, nothing to grasp,
no specific marks, nothing to identify,
neither existent nor nonexistent, beyond real and unreal—
that is what the buddhas intend by 'reflection'.

Colour and form, all sensory perception,
therefore, are like the reflection of the moon in water:
because there is appearance without existence,
because nothing permanent can be found,
because its features, uncongealing, uncrystallizing,
uncompounded, remain but a film of light-form,
the constructs of the eye, the visual faculty and cognition,

suffused by emptiness, are but hollow fictions,
reflections of the moon in water.

We see all things as devoid of truth,
like a ghost, like a banana palm, without a core.

The mind, uncircumscribed, uncontaminated,
uncontrived like the reflection of the moon in water,
simple, empty light-form, unstructured,
we now know as profoundly peaceful, thought-free,
utterly inexpressible primal awareness,
unmoving from the space of its own clarity.

Insofar as the moon appearing in water is not the moon,
so multiplicity as it occurs cannot be substantiated;
free of conceptually imputed divisions of time,*
beyond any conceptual elaboration, let it be, just let it be.

Since pure mind has no purpose whatsoever,
we envision it without outside or inside, beyond thought;
since reality surpasses all invidious, partial distinctions,
we give up the struggle for spiritual capital and status.

Unthought, always a multiplicity, as primordial space,
everything that appears, however it appears,
all things are like the reflection of the moon in water;
not true, not false, samsara and nirvana the same,
let the mind relax into the space of reality just as it is.

---

* Past, present, future; early, earlier, earliest; late, later, latest; punctual, unpunctual; directly, suddenly, gradually; timely, untimely; etc.

The apparent world and all our lives, samsara and nirvana,
are our pictured forms of emptiness, like the moon in water;
nothing in origin, nothing in their advent, nothing in the
moment,
duplicitously imputed by the intellect as true or false, real
or unreal,
why should we cling to opinions and preferences?

So long as the intellect compulsively assumes an ego, or Self,
there is no possibility of release from samsara;
yet beyond belief, naturally settled, in genuine ease,
transparent, transcendent, free in itself and wide open,
the mind egoless, why try to change anything?

When every situation is devoid of ego and substance
like the reflection of the moon in water,
and the intellect free of compulsive activity
and free of habitual presumption about reality,
since in perceptual nonduality mind and its object are one,
this is the space of unmediated, involuntary, Dzogchen.

With a receptivity that takes every occurrence as friendly,
knowing the spontaneity of the cool, nondiscriminating, bliss,
now we are left without anywhere at all to go
and we stay in this pure mind in the primordial ground.

With such realization, abiding in such space,
unerringly, we familiarize ourselves with all experience
as the reflection of the moon in water.
The fortunate person should faithfully recognize
that whatever occurs is a floating, shimmering, mythic reality.

The Meditation

As before, in preparation, aspire to see every moment
as the reflection of the moon in water.
The main praxis is to settle in cognitive sameness,
allowing the mind to perceive what arises
as the reflection of the moon in water.

At night-time, as before, but focus
on the mystical experience of reality
as the reflection of the moon in water;
abiding in unitary space without any clinging
we seize the citadel of the sovereign nature of mind.

Now gazing at whatever appears, free of attachment,
there arises a radiant brightness, the clear light,
that is like the reflection of the moon in water.
Let the supremely fortunate become familiar with that!

Echo: The Sixth Analogy:

Further, the buddhas in their wisdom have said
that all experience is like an echo.
Listen while I clearly elucidate their meaning.

Like a clear echoing voice
returning words spoken at a rock face
all situations are without substance or ego;
we recognize them as unequivocally devoid of truth.

Just as we look for a voice when the echo resounds
and nothing is found outside, inside or in between,
so, also, scrutinizing all experience, inner and outer,
all mental events and the functions of mind,
no trace of a discrete particle, coarse or subtle, can be found.
It is all empty like the sky, immaterial, immaculate,
and recognizing that, grasping and clinging are in vain.

No absolute can be observed in the relative world;
'absolute' and 'relative' are divisive analytic figments:
all in this timeless moment is beyond the intellect.
Knowing the web of structured projections as our own mind,
because the timeless moment cannot now be affected,
the delusory net of constructs has no purchase,
and there is nothing at all to actually grasp and reify.
Knowing that, we go beyond mental projections.

Within this wish fulfilling, skylike, primordial nature of mind
abides an unpolluted ocean of perfectly responsive spontaneity;
due to a loss of presence entailing mental structuring
the fictive mundane world looms absent yet perceptible,
like an echo.

Here, wandering as one of the six mythic modes of being,
self-envisioned perforce by karmically induced propensity,
troubled mind is captured by the fictions that pervade it.

If it is true that living beings and their minds
in actuality are without fundament or base,
how very absurd, the human condition,
perceptible yet non-existent!
What then is the point of our passionate quest for truth?
Why cherish meaning and value where there is none,
in what is seemingly real but actually like echo?
Whatever occurs, just let it be—
it is unreferenced unitary space.
Every adventitious occurrence melts into magnificent unreality,
where, without concern for status, we are foolishly happy.

Whatever occurs, luminous energy without intent,
positive or negative, it is an echo-like event;
whatever it is, it bursts, leaving no trace,
so relax into zero-dimensional unitary space.

Smile lovingly now at these delusive appearances,
at pure evanescence with nothing to hold to,
airy, elusive, disassociated wisps and billows,
flickering make-believe, a glittering phantasmagoria.

Craving truth, the unwise see this all as solid matter;
for the yogin who sees the lie it is unitary space.
Believers who take 'fleeting' as 'lasting' see an eternity;
for those whose belief in eternity implodes it is empty form,
and free of confining conceptual parameters we are happy!

The Meditation

To become familiar with that realization, as before,
in preparation, aspire to recognize echo in all things.
In the main praxis take each experience as empty echo,
for it contains nothing to grasp in the moment it resounds.
Focus concentrated attention in every sensory impression.

All praise and blame, words either sweet or bleak,
are empty sound, with nothing concrete to comprehend;
mind's value judgements all meaningless,
we recognize all these sounds as empty echo.

An angry mind has no location nor dimension,
and evident yet absent, it cannot be found;
it is an empty circumstance, like an echo;
even an enemy's curse, just like an echo.

Scrutinized and found absent, all is empty vibration;
fully apprehended, it is as empty as the sky
where neither good nor bad, benefit nor harm, can occur.
Giving it no credence since in truth it is empty,
we recognize all sound and vibration as enlightening echo.

Thereby, timeless samsaric loads are lifted,
and the fire of anger and hatred is extinguished.
Here we gain sublime patience and avoid wretched depression
and in due course we approach the riches of the buddhas.

At night, as before, focus on the mystical echo experience,
for where sound is empty we acquire patience in life.
Familiarize yourselves with the meaning of echo!

The City of the Gandharvas: The Seventh Analogy

The buddhas in their wisdom have said
that all experience is like a gandharva* city.
Listen while I elucidate the meaning for you
so that you may familiarize yourself with it.

In the sky of primordial clear light, a vision,
a fantastic city of perfectly responsive spontaneity,
abides without beginning or end, centre or boundary.

Out of that plenum of clear light, in our ignorant mind-sky,
created by perceptual duality, lies a gandharva city,
populated by gandharvas—the six mythic modes of being,
variegated colour and form without support or foundation,
born out of the karmically induced propensities of delusory
mind.

Knowing that, we abide in the primordial nature of mind;
in ignorance of it, we are caged in our present delusion.
Since there is nothing concrete to hold on to,
yes, what better analogy than a gandharva city.

Everything, all of it, without intrinsic nature,
is like a gandharva city on a twilight plain,
for both structure and support are delusory.
Comprehended as karmically induced propensity,
deluded mind, now seen as insubstantial,
just let be, bursts and dissolves just as it is.
So, with a strong heart, do not be afraid,

---

* The gandharvas (*driza*) are celestial musicians living in a mythic, illusory city.

For we recognize samsara, pure in itself, as primordially empty.
The objective world, devoid of truth, is a gandharva city;
intellectual constructs, naturally empty, are a gandharva city;
both mind and its quantum field are empty,
like a gandharva city—
let even subliminal beliefs dissolve as they stand.

Undisturbed by the mind, devoid of projections,
whatever situation—absent yet perceptible—arises
although its original delusion arose from compulsive grasping,
now in the moment it may be known in total detachment.

Just as the exalted, immaculate, high of the buddhas—
that perfect peace of nirvana—is utterly insubstantial,
so our own material and immaterial stuff
surely resembles the unreal city of the gandharvas.
Like a vast expanse of celestial space,
we recognize primordial unborn perfect peace.

No desire can be felt there, no anger,
no bewilderment, vanity or envy.
realizing the rational mind to be like a city of gandharvas,
our evanescent emotions, positive and negative,
and the nature of mind—pure mind—are one,
which we recognize as unpolluted skylike sameness.

Samsara has been forever nirvana:
our delusive thoughts evaporate like clouds,
we know the serenity of our original home,
and we cherish this empty clarity
and the perfect peace of primal awareness.

Although that unborn space is free of conventional
perception,
until birth's magical display is enlightened in spaciousness,
we must work to eradicate universal conceptual delusion.
'Doing' and 'not-doing, 'cultivating' and 'abandoning', are one;
but so long as the mind clings to substantiality and the ego-self,
please comply with this deep teaching that counteracts emotion.
We are wise only when we realize the unity of inner and outer
bursting through into the nature of mind.

The Meditation

Now to familiarize ourselves with this reality,
we prepare in the same way as before,
aspiring to recognize every situation as Gandharva City.
The main stance is to clearly identify all colour and form,
empty in appearance, as gandharva cities,
all sounds, smells, flavours, sensations and ideas as gandharva
cities,
all judgements occurring as gandharva cities.
As before, night and day, we accustom ourselves
to everything—whatever appears—as gandharva cities.

Once we see all things confounded with a gandharva city,
letting go in that unreal space, all mental constructs subsided,
self-existent clear light, empty radiance, issues from within.

Likewise, in dream, see it all as a gandharva city
and accustoming ourselves as before to transforming guises
the craving for a permanent identity assuaged,
the chains of perceptual duality are broken
and the propensities that enmesh us completely dissolved
we rest in comfort and ease and attain release.
Familiarize yourselves with the city of the gandharvas!

Apparition: The Eighth Analogy

The buddhas in their wisdom have said
that all experience is like apparitions.
Once again, listen to my elucidation of this truth.

In the space of clear light, our original face,
out of ignorant belief in substance, soul or self,
delusory samsaric appearances emerge.
Like multifarious apparition, absent yet apparent,
we feel them variously as pleasure or pain.

The six mythic modes and their mental environments
are manifested through karmically induced propensity,
but in their purity they are fields of the buddha-trikaya,
autonomous envisionment of clear light and primal awareness.
As the *Net of Transforming Illusion** makes clear
this envisionment has two dimensions—
ordinary mind and primal awareness.

Primordial spaciousness is our universal home,
so pure presence purifying pollution
primal awareness is here and now.
Yet through mental projections of ignorant delusive egotism,
the six mythic modes, happy or sad, appear like apparition.

Like apparitions that appear out of nothing,
we know delusive appearances as pure in their absence;
like an apparition that possesses and controls the mind,
we know the world and its beings as mental infestation;
like apparition that appears according to our caprice,

---

* *Sgyu 'phrul drwa ba*, *mayajala*, a body of seminal Dzogchen texts.

we know every situation is made by causes and conditions;
like delusive apparition absent yet apparent
all situations, absent yet apparent, are mental delusion—
autonomous projections with invasive power—
and conditioned by them, we identify with them.

Breaking through, the habit of reification broken,
we let them be just as they are, and projecting nothing
we abide in the nature of the ground of being,
where, timelessly, the nature of mind is saturated by spaciousness.

The three and five poisons* emanate from mental constructs,
but when scrutinized no substance can be found;
emotion, like apparition, is quite without substance,
so we leave it alone as empty creativity.

All the living beings of the entire universe,
each with physicality, mentality, impulses and feelings,
all are like apparition, absent yet apparent.
They are all unborn, undying, unmoving,
neither engaging nor disengaging,
neither transforming nor changing,
yet they are multifarious appearance.
We recognize them, therefore, as genuine apparition.

The mind's delusory projections with all their pain,
all reside in the space of apparition;
in their absence of substance they cannot congeal,
so we recognize them as nondual empty lies.

---

* Attraction, aversion and dullness; desire, anger, sloth, pride and jealousy.

Phenomena composed of the five elements*—
the triple world and living beings†—
everything, affirmed or denied, are all apparitional mind;
we recognize this mind, absent yet apparent,
as illusory apparition, alpha-pure and pristine.

Everything looks real to the babes,
but intellectually fabricated phenomena and their attributes,
all derived from karmic propensities, cannot be held to be real;
free of perceptual duality that reifies things as 'this' or 'that',
we know it all as inexpressible, boundless openness.

When we verbally indicate a thing as 'this' or 'that',
our words, like rabbits' horns, are hollow names,
mere fictive imputation upon what does not exist:
we recognize all things now as rootless and empty.

What is merely conceptually designated is nonexistent;
imputed by karmic propensity it is absent yet apparent;
and lacking an object the subject expires
so there is no perceptual duality:
it is all unspeakable, unimaginable and utterly open.
Since no one can indicate with certainty, what 'it' really is,
we call it apparition, timelessly without substance or essence.

---

* Earth, water, fire, air, space; solidity, fluidity, heat, motility and dimension.

† The sky, the earth and the subterranean realm populated by gods, men and naga spirits respectively.

Just as in its moment of appearance an apparition is empty,
so all situations whatsoever are empty in reality;
just as an apparition transcends notions of existence,
so the nature of all that arises lies beyond any thought about it.

'Apparent', 'empty', 'true', 'false',
however we label 'it', the label is not it;
letting go of 'this' or 'that'
look into its vast wide-openness.

When there is no compulsive attachment,
whatever arises, that is a totality.
So why covet mere words?
If we believe it to be 'this' rather than 'that'
our natural state of being is diminished.

What can be revealed by a web of speculative concepts?
The mind's imputations are our mental constructs
and even if absolute emptiness could be evoked,
we are left only with belief in the natural state of being.

What can be known by any pointing out,
when the point lies beyond the pointing and the pointed out?
And contentious debate is futile, vain speculation,
and the nature of mind is still unknown.

By virtue of powerful adventitious synchronicity,
the Lama's blessing, however, entering our hearts,
shines like the sublime sun dawning in a cloudless sky,
and in that moment true existential reality is revealed.

All is now unitary space, untrammelled by 'is' or 'is not',
like vast sky, unbounded, unlimited, its emptiness transparent;
now all situations are involuntarily realized as apparition,
empty light-form in vast space.

Whatever is samsara—in this timeless moment—is nirvana,
all delusive concepts realized as the nature of mind;
ego-less primal awareness gambolling in its spacious field,
belief in material appearances now in abeyance,
we are happy in the apparitional space of mind's projections.

With this recognition the Awareness Being sees the truth
and there is nothing left to reveal, for right now, right here,
the nature of mind is bursting through by its own volition.

Yet it is unfolding only in him or her who cherishes
the powerful facility of the guru's blessing.
Colour and form are a blazing lamp to those who can see,
but to the congenitally blind mere words reveal nothing;
whoever is blinded by words, uncomprehending,
he or she cannot see the bright sun of mind's nature.

But blinder than the blind are the scholarly fools,
expatiating like parrots, puffed up by conceit,
the heart-meaning obscured by the web of their concepts,
in their ignorance like the blind in a world of colour.
Unknowing, they believe in the truth of their own thoughts!
Alas! How sad, those most unlucky people! How stubborn!
The heart-meaning always eludes them.

Here, the nature of mind, fearless primal awareness itself,
revealed by the guru, is our actual intrinsic presence.
It dawns when the mind settles, uncontaminated, uncontrived,

in the absence of compulsive attachment to hopes and fears,
but it is best known as unbounded empty clarity.
Whoever has the lineage's blessing, however,
and is caught by the true guru,* he is supremely blessed.

The Meditation
To gain unswerving familiarity with the natural state of being,
as before the preparation is guru-yoga
and aspiration to cultivate experience as apparition.
The main practice is to reinforce experiential conviction
that mind is like apparition,
that the nature of appearances in mind are also like apparition,
that everything is uncontrived, unoriginated, is like apparition.
Let it be in the nature of mind without the slightest agitation.

Now resting in empty clarity free of mental elaboration,
abiding in that space, free of duplicitous perceptual duality,
clear light arises like radiant, translucent apparition.
It's light-forms uncrystallizing, untainted by fabricated beliefs,
it shimmers and glimmers with an unbroken natural happiness.
Skylike mind, its clarity unconceptualized,
knows an unstructured, unelaborated mind-sky.
In this moment all situations appearing like apparition,
the mind's contents released in apparition,
desire and hatred, hopes and fears, the ego, like apparition,
starting point, process and fruition are released.

Here our preconceptions and imaginings no longer bind us:
though fixated on existence all sense of permanence vanishes;
though fixated on nothingness our dirty nihilism evaporates;
though visualizing duality we abide in nondual space;

---

* The true guru is the nature of mind.

though imagining an ego, a soul, a Self, we are free of belief;
conditioned to believe in an alien 'other', now there is no
hope or fear;
cultivating the creative stage, there is spontaneous fulfilment;
cultivating the fulfilment stage, the creative stage is apparitional.*

In its simultaneous arising and bursting emotion is released;
gone beyond subjective belief, we remain in authenticity.
In the chakra of reality temporality is timeless,
and like phantoms we are indifferent to breaks and changes.

The divine madman, aimless, ungrasping, transparent,
in his uninhibited spontaneity has no pretence, no hopes or fears;
whatever appears is unmotivated unitary space,
all-penetrating sky the buddha-dynamic of spontaneity.

Therein, remaining day and night in apparitional space,
all our highs are one in the chakra of pure pleasure;
all our visions total in the chakra of visionary enjoyment;
our every experience embraced in the chakra of reality;
our magical projections incalculable in the chakra of emanation;
and our happiness is sustained in the chakra of protection.

Gross, unreformed, mental energy reduced to essentials—
its structural basis is the system of energy channels,
what is to be purified are the corresponding chakras
and the agent of purification is pure energy;
the actualized purity is the one taste of primal awareness.

---

* The creative stage and fulfilment stage belong to mahayoga and anuyoga respectively.

In dream, our emanation transforms in buddha-fields
and thereafter misleading dreams do not occur.
Staying in the clear light day and night,
in the samadhi of thoughtless clarity and bliss,
clairvoyance, psychic powers, magical faculties
and perfectly responsive spontaneity is achieved.
Now boundless experiences and realizations
for the sake of both self and others are accomplished.
All we fortunate people should unceasingly
familiarize ourselves with all things as apparition!

Concluding Verses

In order to demonstrate the teachings of the buddhas
upon the eight illustrations of magical illusion
I have collected the elixir of sutra, tantra and oral instruction
and expressed them as stainless sunbeams.

Through that virtue may all beings without exception
perceive all situations as unoriginated illusory evanescence,
and achieve higher and higher understanding
beautified by the buddha-trikaya.

Abandoning the intellect that craves security
in what is only dream, magic show, mirage,
reflection, echo and apparition,
let primal awareness and spontaneity regain their primacy.

Once obsessed by the carnal city and emotions,
now fled from the thick jungle of uncertainty
to cool groves far distant,
let the heavens extol and acclaim those babes.

May this, my mind, loathing distraction,
in happy seclusion in the peaceful forest,
focussing only upon real meaning,
achieve the immaculate insight of the exalted.

In this forest of flowers, leaves and fruit,
enhanced by the clear waters of a renunciate lifestyle,
may this my embodiment of unique occasion and right juncture,
walk the path of freedom to the treasure of profound meaning.

In this brief transit, until I attain my goal,
practising virtue in this world of men,
on the path of peace, realizing skilful means,
may I release incalculable beings from this fictive world.

This method is the essence of the buddhas' profound teaching
and as it carries the import of all experiential truth,
with desire for freedom, we should strive from the heart,
day and night, without slackening, living it fully.

Those of later generations, fortunate and faithful,
should depend upon these words at all times,
and crossing over the worldly ocean of self and other,
the dual purpose of all beings is spontaneously achieved.

This yogi with all-penetrating eyes,
seeing the meaning of sutra and tantra
and the essential meaning of all precepts,
Drimey Wozer, graced by stainless radiance,
composed this text in a cave at Gangri Tokar.

This sun of dharma with its myriad stainless rays—
primal awareness shining—dispels the darkness of unknowing,
emptying the ocean of samsara to its last drop,
revealing the unbounded continent of freedom.

APPENDIX I: REALITY ANALOGIES FOR THE 21st CENTURY

A contemporary Nagarjuna would surely include the motion picture as an analogy of this existential maya that unites samsara and nirvana. Perhaps he would include the hologram as another analogy. A contemporary Longchenpa would compose subtle verses tying the analogies to his experience of reality; the verses below are perhaps a pale reflection of them.

The Motion Picture: The Ninth Analogy

The buddhas in their wisdom will say
that all our experience is like a moving picture.
Again listen to the elucidation of that truth.

Mind's nature is like a motion picture,
the film and the screen indivisible.
The moving picture is the magical illusion,
the delusive maya that constitutes our world,
a continuum of pleasure and pain, anxiety and joy.

But the silver screen is cognitive emptiness
remaining untouched by the events it reflects.
Earthquake, tsunami, firestorm, hurricane,

birth and death, love and hate, appear,
yet the screen stays pristine, always immaculate,
never intruding, like the surface of a bright mirror.

The self-conscious viewer,
objectifying the image on the screen,
illustrates delusory dualistic maya
where maya is the foe to be subdued.

But for the movie-goer enrapt in the movie,
like a child engaged in play-acting
yet fully aware of each moment as it turns,
his pristine mind and the movie are at one.
Thus the movie experience is like nondual maya.

Relaxing into that all-embracing cognition,
the picture and the screen are a unitary whole.
Without the screen—no picture;
without the film—just blankness:
the two united—pure joy!

The critical mind observing the movie
discriminates between brilliant and poor direction;
appreciating the good and decrying the bad
he cultivates the karma that determines his rebirth.

In his engrossment in the moving picture,
attached to what comforts, rejecting what dismays,
affirming what pleases and negating what hurts,
his biased propensities are refined and increased.

Believing in the reality of the beings on the screen,
pulled into the magical illusion of the moment,

seduced by the deceptions of movie-maya,
attached to the action as if it were our own,
in turn we laugh and cry, we hope and fear,
captured by the projections created by karmic proclivity.

Believing in the reality of the beings on the screen,
beguiled by make-up and choreography,
by the cunning manipulation of light and sound,
losing sight of the human material underneath,
identifying the actor and actress with their roles
we babes perceive them as real and true celebrities.

When we realize the visual and audio effects are illusory,
that our responses are subjectively determined,
that the scenario of cinema, viewer and movie are delusory,
that the body-mind and its environment are mind-created,
when we relax into the spaciousness of the nature of mind,
either in the movie experience or outside the theatre,
here now is only the flicker of evanescent light-form
and the joy of detachment from every eventuality.

Just as the cinema is an illusory pretence, a fraud, an illusion,
a lie calculated to inveigle and capture its audience,
so the actors are the vehicles and agents of that trick.
To reclaim the awareness and power, value and meaning,
stolen by the apparitions on the screen,
we see all, all as illusion
and thereby we regain our freedom.

Just so, deracinating belief in our 'self',
and belief in the environment as 'other',

the identity usurped by those projections
reverts to its natural state, the nature of mind,
and the maya of false concepts becomes immaculate maya.

The silver screen is populated by self-conscious actors
striving through technique for apparent spontaneity;
in samsara we relax into the nature of mind
through non-action.

The Meditation

To prepare, as before, we aspire to see things as a movie
and the every-day praxis is to gain familiarity with it.
See the events of the waking state as unreal like a movie;
hear all sounds as the sound track of a movie;
hang loosely in the space where everything is unreal already,
free of belief in the reality of our perceptions and conceptions.

The busy mind returns from its peregrinations,
relaxes into the natural state of being,
returns home to the heart centre
and surrenders to the joy of the mind's essential nature.

We are one with the emanation of magical illusion,
the maya of the primal awareness of our being.
Here and now is pure presence, timeless, nondual,
the gnosis that is the heart's desire.

The flow of this moving picture never ceasing,
every instant is complete in itself,
yet inseparable from the whole—
the river-flow training keeps us present.

As in the day so at night: fix the mind in the heart centre
and sleep in the space where dream is like a movie,
and lucid dream, and so on, as before, will certainly arise.

Even visionary experiences and insights are like movie,
and with instinctive recognition of no existents anywhere,
both positive and negative projections collapse.
The eye of insight, psychic powers, samadhis
and perfectly responsive spontaneity are achieved,
and living as buddha we provide guidance to living beings.
Familiarize yourselves with all situations as a movie!

Hologram: The Tenth Analogy

The buddhas in their wisdom will say
that all our experience is like a hologram.
Again listen to the elucidation of that truth.

Just as a hologram is visible but insubstantial
so magical illusion is absent yet apparent;
all our experience is insubstantial delusion,
the maya of false concepts like a hologram,
even immaculate maya like a hologram.

Just as each part contains an image of the whole,
just as a single particle of it contains the entire light-form,
so by knowing a part we know the whole—
we know the universe in a grain of sand.

Like electrons communicating regardless of proximity,
the nature of mind is all-embracing,
each experience an unbounded whole,
space-time as the ground in which it arises.

When its bricks and mortar are empty unitary fields,
space-time is groundless, lacking root or core;
like phantasm, all apparition, like a hologram,
every experience a unitary light-form of mind and its field.

Samsara is an interference pattern, a meaningless jumble,
until illumined by the laser-like light of the mind;
then all our samsaras are nirvana, patterns of light,
like a hologram, awareness of clarity and emptiness.

When a hologram is divided its parts are identical:
like the hologram that is indivisible into discrete parts
so each of the parts of our experience is a whole—
here and now only this unitary light of the mind.

If the particles of a hologram are identical to all others
instant timeless connectivity ensues;
three-dimensional space is a prefabricated illusion
and there are no divisions of time in the here and now

The Meditation
To prepare, as before, we aspire to see all things as a hologram
and the main practice is to gain familiarity with that insight.

First visualise oneself as a hologram,
then include the immediate environment in that hologram
and increase the scope to include the whole world
and finally the entire cosmos with its stars and galaxies.

Experience all the events of the waking state as holograms,
all form as shimmering, scintillating light-form,
abiding where inner and outer, present and absent, are one,
where mind and its transparent creations are only one.

As in the day, so at night: fix the mind in the heart centre
and sleep in the space where dream is like a hologram,
and lucid dream, and so on, as before, will certainly arise.

Even visions and great insights are like holograms.
The eye of insight, psychic powers, samadhis
and perfectly responsive spontaneity are achieved,
and living as buddha we become lamps to all living beings.
Familiarise yourselves with all situations as a hologram!

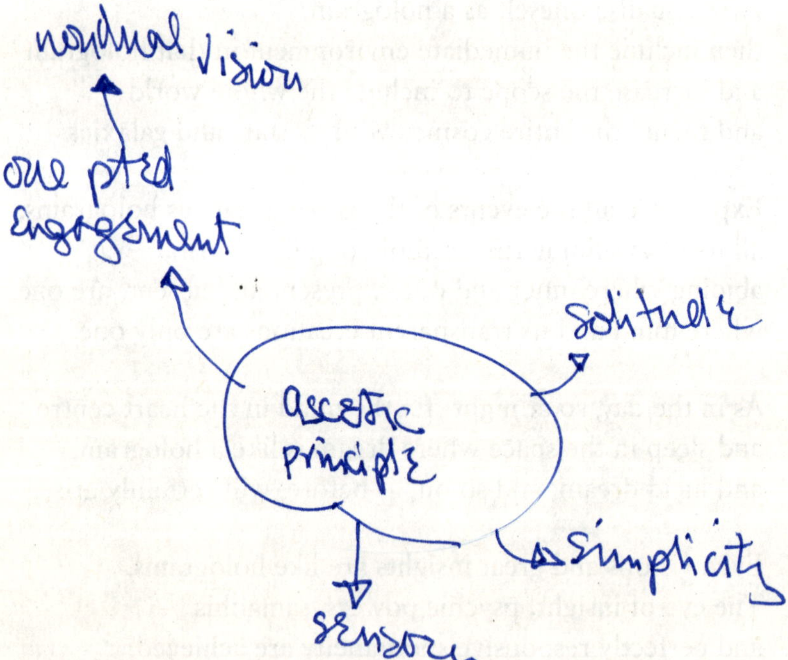

nondual vision
one pted engagement
solitude
ascetic principle
simplicity
sensory reductions

APPENDIX II: CAVE CULTURE

It is easy to infer from the unremitting abstract style of Longchenpa's prose and poetics that he composed his works in the ivory tower of a comfortable monastic academy, served perhaps by unctuous novices compliant to his every whim, visited occasionally by colleagues in awe of his towering achievement. Such a vision may be fitting to Je Tsongkhapa who lived much of his life in hermitages such as Yangon behind Reteng Monastery and Tashi Dokha in Yonlung, forest-grove hermitages set amid the flowering verdure of the lower slopes of the Tsangpo tributaries in Central Tibet. But insofar as much of his life was spent in caves close to the snow line, Longchenpa has more in common with the arch-ascetic Jetsun Milarepa. It is true that Milarepa's caves are located in the High Himalayas at greater altitudes, in the more barren landscape of the northern slopes of the Himalayan range. Longchenpa's caves to the contrary are to be found high in the upper reaches of the side valleys of the Yarlung Tsangpo, where the great river has cut its stupendous gash into the Tibetan plateau allowing the agrarian culture of Central Tibetan to thrive along its banks. Milarepa may have lived the ascetic principle to a greater extreme than Longchenpa, but the essentials of the two lifestyles are the same—solitude, simplicity, sensory reductionism and one pointed engagement in the nondual vision.

Longchenpa's caves, however, like those of Milarepa, should not be pictured as the rough caverns of shepherds or goat herders. It is certain that the caves that both Longchenpa and Milarepa inhabited already possessed a long history of human habitation and that implies shelter—if not immunity—from the elements, with fuel and water supply in proximity. Longchenpa's caves would have been spacious and dry, weather-protected, perhaps with beds carved out of the rock, with a rock-hewn shrine, shelves containing a small library and ancillary space for assistants and guests. A wall across the cave front, perhaps with window and door, may have added to weather protection.

Longchenpa described the ideal exoteric geomancy of a meditation cave. It is situated high at the centre of a half moon arc of hills creating a visual half-mandala, south-facing with a hundred and eighty degree view of the sky, a spring nearby with a tree and a stupa in sight. The location high on a hillside, close to the snowline, is no doubt intended to induce a consciousness of austerity (*tapasya*) but intimacy with spaciousness is still more important. Isolation from the mundane round of village settlement or nomad encampment is ensured but this does not dull the senses or anesthetize the mind. Rather, awareness of the five sensory pleasures is heightened and the tyranny of the internal senses loses its hold. The effect of high altitude on the body-mind insofar as it reduces physical power and the inclination to move the body facilitates a meditative state.

Longchenpa composed *The Trilogy of Finding Comfort and Ease* in the cave hermitage site of Gangri Tokar, lying above the nunnery of Shuksep at the head of the Nyephu valley. Here Longchenpa also composed his great *Seven Treasuries*, the *Khandro Nyingtik* and many other important works. Today the hermitage site is easily accessible by road. A couple of hours of steep ascent from the Shuksep nunnery, through scrub and sparse juniper growth amongst the rocks, takes the pilgrim to the ridge of Gangri Tokar. It is also accessible in a two day walk over yak pastures from the Dorje Drak valley in the south.

The geomantic symbolism of the caves and the mandala aspect provided by the cave at the head of the valley constitute the environmental essentials of the hermitage location. To the west it provides a vista down the valley to the Kyichu river and its meanderings across its flood plain; to the south a magnificent prospect with a view of Riwo Tsenga. But Gangri Tokar lies at the heart of a naturally-manifest image of Dorje Pakmo, the Vajra Sow, formed by the shape of the Gangri Tokar ridge. Two springs generating milky water represent her breasts; Shuksep is on her left knee; and her *yoni* feeds the major stream on the north side of the ridge. Thus the site is replete with natural sacred symbols independent of the artefacts human beings have endowed with sanctity.

The principal power-place at Gangri Tokar is the cave called Orgyen Dzong Wosel Tinkyi Kyemotsel, The Clear Light Cloud Grove of the Citadel of Orgyen. The cave is small and low-roofed, formed by a large overhanging slab of rock walled up at its sides for support. The chapel in front of the cave has been restored. A new small statue of Longchenpa himself has taken pride of place on the cave's altar. Looking out from the cave is the stump of the juniper tree in which resided the guardian deities who assisted Longchenpa with his writing. Close by is the prayer-flag bedecked boulder-residence of the female protectress, Dorje Yudronma, who invited Longchenpa to that spot. Down the slope to the right is the large rock-slab on which Kandromas and Guardians ground down material for ink.

SELECTED GLOSSARY OF DZOGCHEN TERMS

absent yet apparent: med la snang
apparent yet non-existent: med la snang
appearances: snang ba
apply concentrated attention: sgom
buddha-mind: dgongs pa
contaminated: ma dag
defying proposition: spros bral
delusion: 'khrul pa
delusive appearance: 'khrul snang
delusive concepts: 'khrul rtog
duplicitous: bslu ba
efflorescence: rtsal
egoless, without essence: ngo bo med
envisionment, self-envisionment: rang snang
evaluating/judging, affirmed or denied: dgag sgrub
experience: chos
expression: rtsal
false: bden med
familiarization: sgoms pa
free of the intellect's obsessive addictive beliefs: blo yang zhen 'dzin med pa
illusory (nature): sgyu ma lta bu
impure: ma dag

imputation: brtags
intellectual projections: spros pa
labels, signs: brtags
light-form: snang ba
lucid dream: rmi lam zin
maya: sgyu ma
natural state of being: gnas lugs
nature, natural: gshis
no essence to grasp conceptually: ngo bo ngos gzung med
obsessive compulsion, compulsive attachment
identity: 'dzin zhen
passionate belief: zhen 'dzin
perfectly appropriate response: yon tan
phenomena: chos rnams
polluted: ma dag
potency: rtsal
pristine: dag
propositions: spros pa
pure mind: byang chub sems
realization: rtogs pa
reality: chos nyid
recognition: rtogs pa
self-envisionment: rang snang
self-imaged: rang snang
self-sprung: rang byung
simplicity: spros bral
spaciousness: dbyings
specific characteristic: mtshan nyid
spontaneity: lhun grub
synchronicity: rten 'brel
transparent, transparency: zang thal
uncreate: ma skyes
uncrystallized: ma dgag

unelaborated: spros bral
ungraspable, unconcretizable: ngos gzung med
unitary space: phyam gcig
unstructured: spros bral
untrue: bden med
unreal: bden med
value, meaning, benefit: don
wide-open: phyogs yan

SELECTED BIBLIOGRAPHY

H.H. the Dalai Lama. *Mind in Comfort and Ease*. Wisdom: Boston, 2007

Dowman, Keith, *Natural Perfection*. Wisdom: Boston, 2010.

____. *The Eye of the Storm*. Vajra Books: Kathmandu, 2006.

____. *Flight of the Garuda*. Wisdom: Boston, 2003.

Dudjom Rinpoche. *The Nyingma School of Tibetan Buddhism: Its Fundamentals and History*. Two vols. Trans. Gyurme Dorje and Matthew Kapstein. Wisdom: Boston, 1991.

Guenther, H.V *Kindly Bent to Ease Us*, Parts 1-3. Dharma Publishing: Emeryville, 1976.

____. *Jewel Ornament of Liberation*. Shambhala: Boston, 2001.

____. *Philosophy and Psychology in the Abhidharma*. Shambhala: Boston, 1976.

Lingpa, Dudjom. *Buddhahood Without Meditation*. Trans. Richard Barron. Padma Publishing: 1994.

Low, James. *Simply Being*. Vajra Press: London, 1998.

Norbu, Namkhai and Clemente, Adriano. *The Supreme Source*. Snow Lion: Ithica, 1996.

Karmay, Samten. *The Great Perfection*. Brill, Leyden, 1998.

Reynolds, John Myrdhin. *Golden Letters*. Snow Lion: Ithaca, 1996.

Thondup, Tulku. *Buddha Mind: An Anthology of Longchen Rabjampa's Writing on Dzogpa Chenpo*. Snow Lion: Ithica, 1989.

ebook
www.weread.com.np
lost in Transition